Tales From Colorful Lives

Compiled by
Anna Walker

ISBN:1533320470
ISBN-13:978-1533320476

DEDICATION

We dedicate this book to former members of our writing class whose courageous, inspired life stories over the past years have now been completed. They gave us inspiration, encouragement, laughter, tears and endless love in the telling of their tales. The Author and Finisher of our lives has written the conclusion to our friends' autobiographies with these words, "Well done, good and faithful servants." We celebrate the affirmation from Ecclesiastes: "He has made everything beautiful in its own time."

CONTENTS

ACKNOWLEDGMENTS

In addition to thanking our authors for their humorous and heartwarming stories for this edition, this complier would also like to thank a few special people who went above and beyond to help this book to fruition: Thank you to Carole Bos, Pam Martin-Hessel, Laura Monteros, Judy Post, and Norman E. Thomas who edited every story; to Sherman Fung (who painted) and Ken Grant (who drew) our cover; to Pam Miller-Hessel and Judy Post (again) who helped to put final edits into the book; and to Alisha Zuch who took the picture for the back cover.

Where Old Dreams Go
Ken Grant

We have them
Stored Away
Securely locked in
Memory's old closet
Most gathering the
Gentle dust of
Forgetfulness
Though of course
Not all

Like a song once dear
Unsung for many years
That some chance note or
Passing tune may
Resurrect
While we
Perhaps with a smile or
Even an errant tear or two
May break forth
In glad, nostalgic singing!

Many a dream remains
Unshared
In memory's old closet
Too tender for now
And today's hard exposure
Yet remains
A memento of where
Our heart once dared to dream
A beauty that could
Never be
Yet treasured still
In precious memory

A Look Within
Robert Bos

This writing is about us, the residents of Monte Vista Grove Homes in Pasadena, CA. Who are we? It is said that one lady visiting the campus asked a resident, "Are you a nun?" For some, little may be known about those who live behind that big hedge on San Pasqual Street. The words on our bus even announce that we are, "The best kept secret in San Gabriel Valley." At the outset, we are a community of retired pastors, missionaries, and Christian educators. We are a family of faith, the Christian Faith. Included in this are spouses who have served as nurses, teachers, and in other vocations that contribute to the good of society. We are blessed with three levels of living, Independent Living, Assisted Living, and the Health Care Center. The latter two are available to the wider community.

Our grandchildren have been heard to say, "Everyone is so nice here." What finer compliment could be made! They find that people always give them glad greetings and show interest in them, wanting to engage them in conversation. As grandparents we find, too, that a swim in the pool is always a must. The koi pond continues to be an attraction for people of all ages.

As residents, we take a continued interest in not only our children and grandchildren, but the children and grandchildren of our fellow residents as well. They are all part of our extended family. We continue to be interested in their on-going welfare. We want them to be as happy, successful, and healthy as they can possibly be. In our conversations, we ask about them. We celebrate upon hearing any good news or accomplishments, and we feel deeply when we hear of any difficulty they may be facing. We pray for them in our prayer groups.

We are a fragile community. Living here does not make us immune to the problems that others face. There are health concerns: not feeling well, pending surgeries, and uncertain futures. There are down moments but there is seldom a "Woe is me... I am ruined!" spirit (Isa 6:5). There is more of a "comeback spirit". This was evident in meeting a resident in the parking lot returning home from grocery shopping. He was pulling a small cart filled with groceries. We greeted each other with smiles and pleasantries. Both he and his wife had been having major health problems. As he shuffled off with his cane and groceries, moments later I heard him continuing on the sidewalk leading to his home, whistling a merry tune.

We are a caring community. There are those in our number who are younger and agile enough to continue in their service in local churches on a short term basis. There are those, too, who continue to be actively involved carrying out the many volunteer tasks so important to life on our campus. Further, there are countless acts of kindness rendered by residents to residents such as providing transportation, food, writing and speaking words of encouragement, patiently listening to personal worries and concerns. As much as we want to be helpful, it does take a toll on us. At times we need a break and welcome at least brief times away to renew our minds and spirits. We are, however, always happy to return home.

Occasionally, a person on the outside may ask, "What is it like to live in a place where almost everyone is a minister?" Actually, it's stimulating, interesting, and a blessing to be associated with such a remarkable family of people. All agree that Monte Vista Grove is a wonderful place to live. One might even think of it as a little bit of heaven. We are grateful for all that we have here. We are very well provided for and commend the staff who help to make this such a special place. We honor, too, the people who live here. They would be hesitant to tell you about their amazing lives. Most often one doesn't really know until we hear about it in their memorial services. They are preachers, missionaries, chaplains, social workers, educators, innovators, authors, musicians, you name it. This is who they are. They have tried to live effective lives in the name of Jesus Christ by loving and caring for people as they carried out their ministries in this country and abroad.

Living at the Grove can be as interesting and stimulating as one is able or wants it to be. There is a wonderful Wellness program to help keep our bodies and minds strong and active. Many attend noncredit classes on our campus facilitated by Pasadena Community College. Those in the Writing Class write stories of life experiences for their children and grandchildren. Two earlier books of the writings have been published, and this is the third in the series. A music class is designed to offer seniors the opportunity to acquire, expand or improve their musical knowledge and analytic listening skills, while nurturing an enjoyment of a wide variety of musical styles from other cultures. What we know as Convocation and what we call Musings are often interesting and entertaining occasions for the residents and community. Speakers are mostly drawn from the campus and community. Some residents of the Grove find enjoyment in tending their vegetable or flower gardens on campus.

As one who lives here, I would say that we are not perfect by any means. We do have our faults and shortcomings but we try to live in the spirit of love and friendship. In the dining hall we gather around the tables, sitting where there is room. In doing so we sit with different people at every meal. Conversation could arise from a great variety of subjects. At times, loud laughter can be heard and we soon become familiar with the distinguishing laughter of some. Further, there is the enjoyment of warm friendships, the sharing of deep concerns, and the help of loving support. I, personally, am humbled and happy to be a part of this loving, vital community.

As the years pass, there are those of us who more and more succumb to the frailties of old age. What might one expect of a retirement community? The words over one doorway read "This building is dedicated to those men and women who preached the Gospel of Jesus Christ at home and abroad and have come here to rest." We smile, knowing how busy most of us are. Then there is the license plate that reads "Old preachers never die. They Just Pray Away." May our look within reveal a people faithful in prayer and service to their God of love and mercy.

PEOPLE WE'VE MET

The Library Steps
Sherman Fung

We were a foursome -- Bill Chung, Willie Chew, George Huie and myself -- a quartet. Bill was first tenor; I, second tenor; Willie, first bass; and George sang the bottom part of the bass score.

Bill was the oldest in our group. More often than not, he dressed in suits while the rest of us wore casual clothes. He must have worked in an office and had to dress accordingly; in those days that meant a shirt, tie and coat. Bill always looked clean shaven. He combed his moderately thin head of hair neatly, straight back. Even though he was a late-comer to our church group, his former church association made him fit in comfortably with our ways. His tenor voice sounded full and lyrical. He knew all the favorite hymns we young people sang in youth society meetings. "Just As I Am," "Jesus, Savior, Pilot Me," "I Need Thee Every Hour," etc. had no strange words for him. It was a good thing he knew their words well because he had to concentrate on singing the alto line one octave higher. I could only manage the melody.

Willie, who also had a good tenor voice, took the top line in the bass score. Wearing silver rim glasses, he usually had to hold the music closer to his face. Willie was just a class or two ahead of me in the same high school I went to. In fact, he and my older brother, Bob, were in the same grade at Commerce High in San Francisco. Willie was a very good-natured fellow and very capable.

After graduation and before he had a chance to start college, Uncle Sam drafted Willie for World War II. On a visit home after basic training he wanted to marry May Dair, a student in my class and a member of our youth group. Willie asked me to be best man since all his closest buddies were in the service. After the wedding ceremony and reception, the wedding party ended up in a Chinatown nightclub for dinner. The dinner included the floorshow; something we weren't (at least I wasn't) used to: dancing girls cavorting in various stages of dress and undress. If I did not know what nude women looked like, I certainly got an eyeful that evening. After the war, Willie became a next-door neighbor. His wife's mother owned the apartment building next to ours, and the young couple lived in a unit far enough up to escape the racket coming out of the sewing factory in the basement.

George Huie also wore glasses and tended to put his face close to the hymnbook. He handled the bass part usually well. He was somewhat untrained in pitching notes, like me. If it were not for the fact that the soprano line I sang was the melody of the songs we regularly sang at youth meetings, I would be stumbling around trying to hit notes right. George was in the same grade as I was at Commerce High. He was taller and more strongly built than I was. He had thick lips and talked in a low register. That, and swallowing his words, sometimes made him hard to understand, but he had no trouble singing the bass part clearly. I was closer to George than I was to Bill or Willie. Sometimes when I walked George home after church activities, he would invite me in his house to gab some more or to show me something. George had a slew of brothers. I got to know some of them in these informal visits. George also served in the army. After the war he became an auto mechanic with the municipal bus line company.

Did we ever "perform"? To tell you the truth, I don't remember. I do remember we weren't anywhere close to the male quartet on the Haven of Rest radio broadcast. I do remember practicing in the social hall off of the church kitchen with Miss Hubbard at the piano. She played at all our services and meetings, and it was she who encouraged us to sing as a quartet.

The strongest and most lasting image I have of our quartet is the one where we had gathered outside the North Beach Branch Library and conducted an impromptu rehearsal there. For me, that library was a good place to study as well as to do research papers. As life would have it, friends knew that the library was the likely place to find each other. So once and only once, our quartet had a short rehearsal on the steps of the library. That library, even though it was only a branch library -- one located on the outskirts of Chinatown at that -- it did have an imposing staircase. The entrance was set into the front of the upper floor. To reach it from the street, one had to first walk up a set of low steps to a landing and then from there climb the stairs on the right or on the left. These two sets of stairs going in the opposite direction doubled back on themselves along the way and ended up at the broad landing leading to the upper floor entrance. I say "upper entrance" because the library also had a lower entrance off the first landing I mentioned earlier. I had never gone through the doors of this latter entrance. The interior behind this lower entrance was always dark and I never knew what was there. I always thought that there were rooms where books were stored and processed and a place where the staff had rest breaks and lunch. It was only many years later that I learned that that lower level had space large enough to show special films to the public, or to seat an audience for lectures and other programs. I certainly did not have a true, complete picture of things, and I operated on the basis of limited knowledge.

I could not help thinking how my relationship with the members of our quartet was, and is, so much like my relationship with the North Beach Branch Library. Bill? I don't know what happened to him. He just disappeared as all of us went our separate ways. Maybe he popped back to his hometown as suddenly as he appeared among our youth group. Willie? He went up the ladder professionally from ESL teacher in Francisco Junior High School to Supervisor of ESL programs for the Board of Education in San Francisco. I was saddened to learn that he and May divorced. Willie did eventually remarry a Caucasian woman. He kept an increasingly peripheral relation to the Chinatown church. George? I supposed he stayed with the city bus company until retirement. He married Isabel, the sister of another George in the church. In fact, this second George was the person who introduced me to the church in the first place and got me started on my journey of faith.

O yes, the library steps. Whether you use the right set or left set of stairs to go up or come down, you ended up the same place together. Maybe life will be like that too in the end. No matter how separate our ways, we may still get together again.

The Measure of a Person
Barbara Mathieu

Jok Madut Jok was born in a rural village of South Sudan, between 47 and 53 years ago. He was the second of six sons born to his mother Angeth and his father Madut Dit in the cattle-keeping Dinka village of Marol.

Around the age of ten, young Jok was aware that because his mother had only sons, there was no daughter to help her with the women's work. She arose before sun-up to pound the sorghum for the daily meal of porridge. At first light she went to fetch water in the large pail she would carry home on her head. The next task was to collect firewood for the fire over which she would cook the porridge.

She would see to getting the school-aged children ready to walk the 4 kilometers to the nearest school, then return to stir the cooking porridge to be eaten in the afternoon after their school day was over.

Jok decided he would be his mother's helper since she had no daughters. He got up before sunrise to help her. As soon as he was noticed doing "girls' chores", he was derided mercilessly by the males of his village—even his own father who had taught his sons that "The measure of a person is how he stands for others"! His uncles, cousins, and elder brother all criticized and taunted him for doing the chores of a girl.

One day after a particularly rough time of harsh criticism, Jok told of his grandmother putting her arm around his shoulder and tenderly whispering in his ear, "Jok, you will be a better man because you understand the world of women"!

Jok's doctoral dissertation from UCLA's School of Public Health and Anthropology is entitled "How War Affects the Reproductive Health of Women."

He opened a school for girls, the Marol Academy Primary School, in his home village in 2008 to honor his deceased mother. In a country where there had been no school due to over two decades of civil war, three hundred and thirty youngsters showed up the first day. Today, eight years later, over eight hundred girls and boys are enrolled.

I chair the Board of Directors for the non-profit organization supporting Professor Jok's village school project.

The Greater Risk
Bruce Calkins

Today, when you hear a recorded speech by Martin Luther King Jr., you feel the depth of his commitment to overcoming the power of hate with the power of love. But I want to tell you, when you heard Dr. King in the 1960's, you'd get a lump in your throat; you knew you were listening to a man who was standing in the cross-hairs of the sights on a rifle.

King spoke to a people who were *also* in the cross-hairs.

As I listened to King in Washington on August 28, 1963, my breathing got faster; my skin tingled. I knew there were people out there who used lynchings and beatings as a method of control. I thought, "How can he be so direct and forceful and honest when it's so dangerous?"

I was near the reflecting pool in front of the Lincoln memorial, and I remember how I felt when he got to the part of his speech where he said, "Let freedom ring from the mighty mountains of New York." Then he mentioned the hills of Pennsylvania, the mountains of Colorado, and the curvaceous peaks of California! I thought, "Yes, he's calling for freedom and justice in the North, where we like to pretend that we are more just."

Then he went on, "Not only that; let freedom ring from Stone Mountain of Georgia! (We all cheered.) Let freedom ring from Lookout Mountain of Tennessee! Let freedom ring from every hill and every molehill of Mississippi!!" He mentioned Georgia and Mississippi by name!

We cheered, but I also shivered. You just don't say things like that out-loud. I could imagine someone in Mississippi reaching above his mantel and taking down a rifle. King knew it was dangerous to speak like that. He also knew it was dangerous to keep silent!

Later, I heard him speak in Brown Chapel in Selma, Alabama. The clergy who had come to Selma after "Bloody Sunday" were asked to sit on the platform with King; so, there he was right in front of me.

He was always way out in front of all of us.

7

His words in Selma were calm. He didn't need to inspire the marchers to action. He wanted to be sure that we would be peaceful. However, the atmosphere was not peaceful. There'd been a killing nearby recently.

Another white pastor who had come to Selma decided to go and talk with some of the white citizens of Selma. He asked them what they thought about all this. He hoped to be able to soften their hearts a little. Word traveled fast. As he started to cross a street, a pickup raced around the corner. It was aimed right at him. He jumped back just in time. The driver laughed as he roared past.

King knew the risk of crossing the Edmund Pettus Bridge and then marching to Montgomery to demand the freedom to vote. He also knew the danger of doing nothing.

After the assassination of President Kennedy, Dr. King and his wife Coretta attended Kennedy's funeral. During the service, King leaned over to Coretta and said, "Someday that'll be me."

Coretta said, "I know."

King went on to Montgomery and then to Memphis; because the risk of silence was greater than the risk of action.

I see in Martin Luther King Jr. as a man who lived the words of Jesus who said: "No one has greater love than this, to lay down one's life for one's friends." (Jn. 15:13 NRSV)

The Norman Thomas
Norman E. Thomas

I do not remember when I first realized that I had the same name as a famous person. **The** Norman Thomas was the Socialist candidate for President of the United States in 1928, '32, '36, '40, '44 and 1948.

Probably my parents voted for Norman Thomas. They must have spoken positively about him. At least by age eight I knew of **the** Norman Thomas.

The *National Geographic* magazine stimulated my interest in far-away places during my childhood years. Mother and Dad subscribed to it and all the family enjoyed it. In earliest years I feasted on its pictures of glaciers, wild animals, and peoples in exotic lands. About age eight I began to clip coupons in the *Geographic* and send away for free travel literature.

One day the phone rang and I was the first to answer it. To my "Hello" came back the response: "Are you Norman Thomas?" "Yes," I replied. "Mr. Thomas," the caller continued, "I am your Grace Line representative. I have called to assist you in planning for your South America cruise." Putting down the phone I called out for help "Mommy!" Fortunately, Mother was nearby in the kitchen and came to my aid, explaining to the caller that this was not the home of **the** Norman Thomas, the politician.

The Norman Thomas

Twelve years later, during my undergraduate studies at Yale, I got to meet **the** Norman Thomas. He was speaking at the university. Sidney Lovett, Yale's chaplain and long-time friend of Thomas, probably got me an invitation to the dinner in Thomas' honor. My first impression was of a distinguished-looking man with receding silver hair. Someone took me up to meet him. I introduced myself as Norman Thomas. In our short but animated conversation I retold the story of being confused with him at the age of eight. He responded with a story that he had been confused with the Negro pianist Norman Thomas. Later I learned that this Norman Thomas had performed in Harlem, and released a Vitaphone recording in 1929 entitled "The Norman Thomas Quintette in Harlem-Mania."

"Are you related to **the** Norman Thomas?" That's the question asked repeatedly of me by strangers during my adult years. "No," I would respond patiently. "I am named for my uncle Norman on my mother's side."

Sometimes the inquirer would next share feelings about Norman Thomas the Socialist. Some said that they voted for him. In response I shared that my parents deeply respected him and may also have voted for him.

Years passed. Those that I spent in southern Africa from 1961 to 1976 offered a welcome relief from that ice-breaking line of conversation with strangers. I was on a continent where the history of internal politics in the USA was as unknown as those of African states are in the USA.

I returned to the United States in 1976; **the** Norman Thomas had died in 1968. Most persons born after 1940 had not heard of him unless well-read on 20th century US politics. With decreasing frequency came that query, "Are you related to **the** Norman Thomas?" I even tested a new response to the question: "I am **the** Norman Thomas."

But in 2006 the old question, "Are you related to **the** Norman Thomas?" re-emerged when I moved to Monte Vista Grove in Pasadena, California, a retirement community for workers of the Presbyterian Church, USA. They all remembered **the** Norman Thomas for he had been a Presbyterian minister. Upon graduation from seminary he could have pastored the affluent Brick Church on New York's 5th Avenue. Instead, he chose to minister in East Harlem among the poor, in the district that had the highest homicide rate in the city. It was déjà vu for me as patiently I repeated my answer given so often fifty years earlier: "No, I am not related to **the** Norman Thomas. I am named for my uncle Norman on my Mother's side."

Retirement has given me time to read about the life of my namesake. In doing so I deepened my appreciation of him. Thomas was the nation's most visible Socialist from the 1930s through the 1960s. Often he was called "America's conscience."[i] Martin Luther King Jr. wrote to him: "I can think of no man who has done more… to inspire the vision of a society free of injustice and exploitation… all that we hear of the Great Society seem only an echo of your prophetic eloquence."[ii]

In 1932 Thomas shaped the Socialist platform. It favored public works, a shorter work week, agricultural relief, and unemployment insurance. Its planks included the elimination of child labor. It advocated for old-age pensions, slum clearance, low-cost housing, and higher taxes on corporations and the wealthy.[iii] When Franklin Delano Roosevelt won the presidency in a landslide, Norman Thomas received 884,781 votes—2% of the total. In later elections he lost even this level of popular support. Within fifty years the United States had adopted every one of those 1932 proposals while retaining its capitalist economy. That's why I now respond to the question: "Are you related to **the** Norman Thomas?" "No, but I am proud to bear the same name as that famous American."

[i] Peter Dreier, *The 100 Greatest Americans of the 20th Century: A Social Justice Hall of Fame* (New York: Nation Books, 2012), 138.

[ii] Ibid, 141.

[iii] W. A. Swanberg, *Norman Thomas: The Last Idealist* (New York: Charles Scribner's Sons, 1976), 135.

The Silent Angels of Oban
Bill Hansen

On our first visit to Scotland we found Edinburgh the most beautiful city that we had ever visited. From our lodgings I drove several nights into Princes Street just to view the spectacle of the lighted spires and towers that punctuate the rise of High Street across the way. High Street rises from the Palace at the bottom of the hill to the topmost edge where the Castle stands. From the advantage of Princes Street, the whole city of Edinburgh sparkles like a multi-faceted Disney Land. At night especially, the scene is breathtaking.

The next day we traveled north from Edinburgh to make a full day's journey to the small western coastal resort town of Oban. Oban is a center for fishing and for holiday bound tourists. We arrived at Oban very late in the afternoon. We did not realize that the weekend was a special holiday in Scotland. The picturesque Oban harbor, surrounded by the Scottish hills, was crowded to the hilt with visitors. As we set about locating a bed and breakfast for the night it became obvious that there were no vacancies to be found anywhere. We stopped at the last hotel along the breakwater and realized that we might not find lodging for the night. As a last resort we stopped at the local visitors' center where reservations can sometimes be made. Standing at the end of a long line we discovered that our search was hopeless. An official advised us to drive south along the coast where we could find several small villages where there might be accommodations. He emphasized the word MIGHT!

In the failing light of evening we headed south on a two lane road that narrowed quickly into little more than one lane leading south. The dense deciduous woods closed in along the roadway. We drove for forty minutes or so but we found no village nor even houses along the way. We were driving a small rented Morris Minor and at that point in the distance ahead, I could see another car approaching. It appeared to be coming at a racing speed. The road was barely one lane in width and to avoid a collision I suddenly turned off the lane onto what appeared to me to be a lush green shoulder. Unfortunately, the lush green shoulder actually proved to be a deep ditch covered by a tall growth. We came to a sudden halt as I turned off the road. I discovered that we were balanced on the edge of a deep drop off. Our rear wheels were unable to get traction and it was obvious that we were now stuck on the edge of a deep ditch. The other car stormed by.

As I sat immobilized behind the wheel in the drivers' seat I realized that we were surrounded by deep woods. There was nothing in sight – not a sign of civilization anywhere. The light was failing rapidly and I wondered what might be our next move.

I was about to climb out of the little car when all of a sudden, silently from out of the woods 6 or 7 young Scotsmen appeared. They didn't say a word to us but silently they surrounded the car with both of us still in it. They picked up the whole little car! They put us back on the road and just as silently as they had appeared, they turned to walk away and disappeared into the woods. I got out of the car and tried to thank them. One just turned and waved to us and they were gone.

Gratefully we turned around and headed back to Oban. We arrived once more at the visitors' center well after dark. The center was empty now except for the woman behind the desk. The other tourists had given up the wait. As we entered she recognized us, her face lit up and she said, "Your timing couldn't be better. I just received a call from a sea captain's wife. Her husband is a sea and she heard that there were many who were stranded without lodging. She said she would open their own bedroom to a visitor just for tonight."

The captain's bedroom turned out to be in a luxurious home. It was perched on a hillside with a commanding view of the tall masts of the ships in the harbor below. The bedroom was beautifully furnished with a bay window overlooking the rugged seaside landscape.

We rose early the next morning to keep reservations on the small boat that would sail for the historic Island of Iona. It was from this remote monastery on Iona that the monk Columba had evangelized Scotland and planted the Celtic Church in Scotland. That morning in Oban the sea captain's wife served us a hearty breakfast before we left for the dock to catch our boat to Iona.

The trip to Iona was unforgettable – inspiring and indescribably meaningful.

Our visit to Oban, including the sea captain's wife and the 6 mysterious young Scotsmen provided an experience that was never to be forgotten! Of course we will never forget…

THE SILENT ANGELS OF OBAN.

The Last Dance at the Rendezvous Ballroom
Bill Hansen

When I was a college student in the late 1940's the places to dance in Southern California were the Palladium in Hollywood, the Trianon Ballroom in Los Angeles, the Avalon Ball Room on Avalon Bay at Catalina Island, and The Rendezvous Ballroom at the foot of the Balboa Beach Pier. There were other popular places to dance but the Big bands, like Glenn Miller, Artie Shaw, Harry James, The Dorsey Brothers, Paul Whiteman and Lionel Hampton all played in the ballrooms that I have mentioned. The Pavalon on the pier at Huntington Beach was played by lesser bands the best of which I remember was "Les Brown and his Band of Renown". There were some fairly good "Wannabe Big Bands" that the Pavalon featured on Friday nights like a local beach band whose leader was Jack Rose. During the summer sometimes we would take in dances on both Friday and Saturday nights. Usually on Friday nights we went as a gang and Saturday nights were for dates.

At a funeral twenty or so years ago as a pastor I had occasion to remember the Pavalon. I arrived at the Westminster City Cemetery a little early so I checked in at the chapel where the service was to be held. The City of Westminster is on the outskirts of Huntington Beach. Inside the Chapel a woman of ample girth was at the organ... let me just say that she most generously overflowed the organ bench. She was very enthusiastic when she found that I had grown up in the summertime at Huntington Beach, and that also as a college student I had danced at the Pavalon.

"Do you remember the Jack Rose band?" she asked.

"Absolutely," I said, "they played on Friday nights and they were pretty good!" The woman beamed. She virtually leaped from the organ bench, thrust her arms out in a staged pose and announced "Then you'll remember me... I'm BUBBLES!!!"

It turned out that I did remember her. She played piano and from time to time would run around behind the band and blow Bubbles into the air from a Bubble Pipe. She said that Lawrence Welk once heard the Rose Band, liked her idea of the Bubbles and actually paid her for his bands' use of Bubbles! I have no reason to believe that her story wasn't true. To tell the truth, I can't remember today the name of the person for whom I conducted the funeral that day, but I still remember Bubbles!

The Rendezvous was our favorite place to dance. When the band took an Intermission, you could walk out onto the Balboa Pier into the briny evening air, cool off and walk with your date under the stars with the sound of crashing waves and the light of the moon reflecting from the luminous white water of the breakers. At the end of the pier you could buy a coke, lean against the railing of the Pier, stand close together to ward off the chill of the air, and talk about anything that came to your mind except school studies of course. After the intermission you were ready to dance again. There was jitterbug, the Balboa two step, once in a while the Charleston (although that was our parent's dance) and toward midnight there would be a conga line. Then slow dancing and waltzes...and then inevitably at 2:00 in the morning at the last dance the whole band would sing:

"Good Night Ladies, Good Night Ladies, Good Night Ladies, We're Going to Leave You Now!"

There was one evening in the summer of 1949 at the Rendezvous Ballroom on the Balboa Pier that proved to be most memorable for me. Lionel Hampton was playing for only one night and it was Saturday. I am sure that the ballroom was crowded way beyond fire department mandated capacity that night. The crowd was more high spirited than usual because Dean Martin and the Rat Pack were there. They had arrived not at all anonymously on their Harley Davidsons. The beat and the tempo of things kept building through the evening, and the temperature in the hall was made more intense by the overly crowded dance floor. The atmosphere became more and more intense and the volume and the beat of the Hampton Band reverberated from the ceiling and the walls and the floor.

Obviously those who left at the intermissions returned having consumed more than pure coke in a glass. Finally, couples weren't even dancing together any longer. Instead groups of five or even ten were forming - arms wrapped around each other's shoulders. The sound of feet pounding the floor and the hypnotic beat of the band and the heat gave the impression of a crowd that was losing control. Lionel Hampton and the band seemed oblivious as they continued to drive what now seemed like a frenzy.

I had gone with my beach friends in a group that night. Somehow we managed to seek each other out in the crowd. One of us pointed to the exit that led out onto the pier. We pushed and shoved our way through the dense crowd to the exit and then spilled with relief out into the night air onto the Pier and then we piled into our parked station wagon. We admitted later that it had been a little crazy and we were glad to be on our way home. We left at 1:00 in the morning.

The Lionel Hampton dance ended at 2:00 that morning. Thankfully, it ended before there was a riot. But that night proved to be the last dance that was ever held at the Rendezvous Ballroom on the Balboa Pier. Police suspected, but could never prove arson. The Rendezvous burned down that night, burned to the ground, and it was never rebuilt.

The Palladium, the Avalon, the Trianon, even the Pavalon carried on for several more years until the era of the big bands itself began to fade. But one by one, like the Rendezvous, the great dance halls and ball rooms of Southern California, and the big bands themselves, with just a few exceptions all played their LAST DANCE. A bit like the night of the last dance at the Rendezvous Ballroom.

Oscar
Mae Gautier

I didn't understand why the colored people should have to come in the back door, but I was powerless in that situation. Not only was I little, but I was also a girl.

Oscar was tall, lanky, very black, and worked for a multitude of Gautier families all his life….well, nearly all of his life. They said he didn't know his age and that he couldn't read or write, which may be true, but maybe not. He didn't talk much; didn't talk much to us, that is. He would talk with other colored people.

I have said "colored people" twice now. The other word we knew was "nigra", a "nice person's" way to say Negro and to avoid "nigger".

Mama said they thought Oscar was about her age because he showed up in Miami from the Bahamas about the time she married Daddy in 1912 and he seemed about her age, 16.

Besides our house, he worked at Grandma's, Aunt Theda's and Uncle Lawrence's, Cousin Ida's and Cousin Redmond's, Cousin Robert's and his wife's, Great Aunt Mary's and Mary Louise's, and others. I don't remember the names of the rest any more, but they all were Gautier families.

Oscar worked at our house two mornings a week: some house cleaning, some grass mowing, and occasionally, maybe twice a year in an evening, helping with a special dinner. For example, when Mama invited the new preacher and his wife for dinner.

Oscar lived, of course, in what was known as "Colored Town" in a rented room. There were a few colored towns in various parts of the Miami area. We lived in the near southwest and Oscar lived in Colored Town (known now as Liberty City). What an irony! It is around northwest 15th Street and Miami Avenue as I remember it, and was the Colored Town nearest our area.

I think Oscar never had the money for bus fare or perhaps he was self-conscious of his bad smell. Anyway, he walked from his house to all our various Gautier houses. To our various Gautier back doors, that is. I did hate that. I didn't care if he smelled or didn't talk or was illiterate. My Sunday School teacher, Mrs. Frost, the preacher, Rev. Allen, and Mama and Daddy and Aunt Theda and Uncle Lawrence, and the rest of them, said I was to be like Jesus who loved everyone, "red and yellow, black and white". I would think: What's wrong with you two-faced people? And think their answer: Well, ahem! God made us different, and well, ahem, … some are black and smell and have to come in the back door …and that means they should not come in the front door, etc. That's all... As I said, I was powerless because I was young, and only a girl.

Back in 1930, when I was born, the Depression had hit us all, Oscar included. Sink or swim, we'd stick together, sharing what we had, and that included Oscar "Gautier". He was always given work and always given food to eat, and some amount of money.

I tried to be friendly with Oscar, but he didn't want that. It most certainly would not be OK for him to play with me. Except, he did have one kind-of-a-game he played with me. He would take a huge step toward me, lean down and say in a stage-whisper, "M-A-Y May, M-A-Y May". "No, no, it isn't", I would yell, jumping up and down. It's "M-A-E. Mae". We'd repeat…

His name, I learned later, was Oscar Perpal. Because the hero of the times, Franklin Delano Roosevelt, got us social security, Aunt Theda, in the '40's, got it for Oscar, and, of course, she needed his name for that. It is Oscar Perpal. As far as I know, all the families paid in on the social security.

And then, after all those years, Oscar retired when he was about 73. As Oscar Perpal he retired to his homeland, the Bahamas, and with his social security he built a concrete block house for himself. My sister found a way to locate him. She and her husband went to the Bahamas and, after a big search, they found where he lived and visited him...at his own house.

This is My Life: Sonia Leiva
Howard Den Hartog

For the past fourteen years I have worked as a CNA in the memory care facility at the Solheim Lutheran Home in Eagle Rock, a neighborhood area in northeast Los Angeles, California. I enjoy what I am doing. Four years ago we received a new patient, Esther. Her room is in the same area of the memory care unit where I work so she became my charge. Since I work the morning shift, I get her up in the mornings, bathe her, clothe her, put make-up on her, feed her breakfast, etc. She just melted my heart beginning on the first day of her arrival. Her warm, friendly smile and sparkling blue eyes made it a joy to be her nurse. Her husband, Howard, came to visit her every day during the noon hour. Because she does not eat, he took it upon himself to feed her. Over time when he came to visit Esther, we would carry on conversations with each other. We talked about many things, like where we were born, our families, how much schooling we had—the list goes on. Finally one day Howard said to me, "Sonia, you should write your history." He kept encouraging me. "Sonia, write your history, write your history." I had never done anything like that before. My English is not as good as I would like it to be, but finally one day I said, "Okay, I will do it."

I was born on July 19, 1978 in the city of Berlin, El Salvador, in the department of Usulutan. A department is like a state in the United States. My father's name is Pedro A. Portillo Dominguez and my mother's name is Gloria Leiva. When I was six months old and my brother, Remberto, was two years older, my mother left home and went to live in the United States. She told my grandparents when she had enough money, she would come and get me and my brother. That never happened. Down through the years I do not remember having any correspondence with my mother. When I was older, she told me she sent money to my grandparents. I did not see my mother again for fourteen years. Immediately after my mother left, my father took my brother and me to his parents to live. He moved into the city to work. He would visit us once in a while but not very often so I never got to know him very well. My grandparents became my parents. They gave us lots of love and took very good care of us. Their names were Maria Portillo and Pedro Antonio Dominguez. My grandfather was a hard worker. He was a carpenter, brick and tile layer, roofer, and in general construction. He worked mostly for rich people. We lived in a small modest home with two bedrooms, living room and a kitchen. My grandmother did most of her cooking outside and used wood for fuel. My favorite foods growing up were pupusas and tamales. My mama made four kinds of pupusas: pork, beef, bean, and cheese. She began by making a small ball of corn flour with her hands, then made it into a small round tortilla. The pork was ground until very thin. Then she put it in the middle of the tortilla, flattened it and cooked it over a fire. Oh, they were good!

I began school when I was five years old. We all wore uniforms to school. Our skirts were green and our blouses were white worn with a black necktie. Each school had a different color uniform so you could tell which school the students attended. It was around the time I began school when my seven-year-old brother Remberto suddenly died. That was a sad time for me. We had so much fun playing together. That was my first experience with death and I was really too young to comprehend it all. I do remember being lonesome, not having him around to play.

When I was fourteen years old, my mother came to see me. I did not know her because she left when I was just a baby. She wanted me to come to the United States to go to high school. She told me she would come back in another year because she did not have all the paper work done. I did not know what to think, but it sounded exciting. I arrived in the United States two weeks before my fifteenth birthday. The moment I arrived I became homesick. I did not know anyone and had no friends. I could not speak English and everything seemed different. My mom did not seem like my mom because I really did not know her as a mother. I now had a five-year-old stepsister Lourdes whom we call Lulu and a stepbrother Cesar. School was hard because I did not know any English. Every night I cried myself to sleep. Cesar got caught up with the gangs. When he was seventeen, he was shot and killed. I did poorly in school and could not keep up. This went on for three years; I begged my mother to let me go back to El Salvador. Finally she consented. I was around eighteen years old and I was happy again. I had my friends and I was determined to get my high school diploma which I did even though it took me three years. I was a good student but I studied hard to earn it. That was a happy time in my life. My mama and papa were proud of me. During these three years I lived with my mother's parents. I went to parties with friends, and we danced which is a large part of my culture. Our theater was destroyed during the civil war so we could not attend movies, but we had TV.

Then something happened for which I was not prepared. After graduating from high school I became pregnant. I became very scared and confused. What was I going to do? I had no job and no money. How could I support myself and a baby? I didn't think it would be fair to live with mama and papa, and I knew how hard it would be to try and make a living in San Salvador. I didn't know how to tell mama. Finally I got up enough courage to talk with her. We both cried. I also talked with my mother who invited me to come back to the United States and live with her which I did. This whole ordeal really made me grow up fast, but I still had a lot of soul-searching to do. How would I learn English? Where would I live? Would I be able to get more schooling? Before my baby, Gloria, was born, I made some big decisions. The United States is where I was going to live and I wanted to become a citizen. I discovered that in order to become a citizen I had to pass a test and live in the United States for five years. I studied hard to learn English. Finally, I took the test and passed. I became a citizen on December 9, 2007. That is an important day in my life.

I lived with my mom around a year after Gloria Stephanie was born. She has my mother's name. Then I lived on my own. That was tough and my income was small, but I survived. One job I had was at Taco Bell. Oh, I hated that job. I did not want to clean houses; I wanted to do something I enjoyed. Along the way I took classes to be a CNA. My mom was working at Solheim as was my Aunt Isabell, my mom's sister. I applied and was accepted. I have been there now over fourteen years and I love my work. This is where I really became fluent in English, talking with my patients. My goal is to go back to school, get a LPN license and hopefully someday go to college.

Eight or nine years ago I met Raul Zelaya. He began working at Solheim in the maintenance department. We became close friends and lived together for almost six years, but our relationship did not last. He is the father of our daughter, Ashley Michelle Zelaya, born August 10, 2009 and a son, Raul Alexander Zelaya, Jr. born October 10, 2011. My daughter, Gloria Leiva, is sixteen years old and was born November 29, 1999. She is a junior at Highland High School in Highland Park, a neighborhood northeast of Los Angles. She is in ROTC and loves it, wearing her uniform to school.

It is common in the Hispanic culture for a girl to have a Quinceanera celebration when she becomes fifteen years old. I put away some money each month so Gloria could celebrate that special day. It was a beautiful day and just a wonderful celebration. Gloria looked beautiful. My Aunt Martha, my mom's sister, even flew from Houston, Texas. A Quinceanera celebrates a girl passing from childhood to womanhood.

When I was in El Salvador, I took my mother's maiden name for my last name instead of my father's last name. This is where Gloria gets her last name, Leiva. In El Salvador unmarried women must use their first name, middle name, mother' maiden name and father's last name when signing important documents. Since I took my mother's maiden name I would not use Dominguez, my father's last name.

I went back to El Salvador when I was eighteen and I saw my father a couple of times. I have not seen him since. About a year ago, through Facebook and telephone calls, we finally reconnected. Now we talk with each other once or twice a month. I am anxious to see him again.

Several years ago I saved enough money to buy a used BMW, a rich man's car. I loved to drive it and had it over ten years. Now I have a 2003 Toyota.

I am now thirty-eight years old. I love my family. The last four years my mom and I have become especially close to one another. She loves her grandchildren. I am happy and enjoy life. Last but not least, I am grateful to Howard for encouraging me to tell my life story.

- -

The above story was written by Howard Den Hartog over a period of several years and numerous conversations.

This is My Life
by Felipe...a loving pet
1997-2014

Nathaniel, this is my 2012 Christmas present to you....

Last week the arthritis in my legs was bothering me so I did not feel up to walking the two miles with Grandpa so I just stayed in bed. Instead of going to sleep until Grandpa returned, I began to think about what I could get you for Christmas. I decided I would write you a story of my life and entitle it, "This is My Life." I have always enjoyed having my picture taken so I have put together a photo album to go along with my life story.

I was born February 25, 1997, on the west side of Salt Lake City, Utah. I had a loving and caring mother along with several brothers and sisters. I could not have asked for a better home in which to be born. When we were around six weeks old, we were told we would all be adopted and have a new home. An ad was put in the paper and many people came to look us over. I will never forget when you and Grandpa and Grandma came to see us. I knew right away, Nathaniel, when you picked me up and cuddled me so gently that I wanted to be your companion. I was so happy and thrilled when you told the lady you would purchase me. The next day you came and picked me up and I was so excited. I just knew we would be a perfect match for one another. I enjoyed living in Salt Lake City the next couple of years. Not too long after I came to live with you, Grandpa and Grandma purchased Powder Puff. She was the joy of my life. We had so much fun playing together. We would chase one another around the house until we were dead tired. Powder Puff's favorite game was to hide behind the couch or wall and then pounce on me when I came running into the room. We would roll and tumble over each other. What a fun time we had together. Sometimes I thought I was a cat and she thought she was a dog. Those days together are precious memories.

I was overjoyed again when you brought Angel to live with us. I remember it was so much fun when you took us on walks through the neighborhood. Powder Puff and I really hit it off. I will never forget the day when you, Angel, and I were playing in the front yard. Angel began to chase a leaf a strong wind was blowing down the sidewalk. The leaf just kept going and going and Angel kept chasing it. Then it happened. Angel chased the leaf into the street, and not thinking to look to see if any cars were coming, was struck by a car. My whole world caved in on me. What would I do? I was over-whelmed with grief. You took me in your loving arms, Nathaniel, and caressed me and told me that now Angel would be in puppy heaven. At night I would quietly cry within my heart. That was my first experience with death. It took me weeks to recover; I was so sad.

I recall that almost immediately after I came to live with you, you began to teach me to do many things. You kept telling me how smart I was because I learned so fast. I loved to do tricks and perform for family and friends. Through the years you taught me how to shake hands, roll over, pray, crawl, sit up, play dead after being shot, play basketball, play hide and seek, jump up and down, and fetch Grandpa's house slippers. When we lived in Salt Lake City and Grandpa was working for the church, I always looked forward to his noon hour. After lunch he took a nap on the couch. Powder Puff, Angel and I would sleep on top of him. Also, I loved helping Grandpa lock the church at night. I would run ahead of him and wait for him to catch up. I knew the route by heart.

When Grandpa and Grandma retired in 1999, moving all of their belongings to Sisters, Oregon, I felt I had become a world traveler. We all rode in that huge motor home, pulling the U-Haul trailer. After two or three long days we finally arrived in Sisters. I loved the smell of the ponderosa pines the moment we arrived. I never dreamed that years later Sisters would be my home again before moving to Monte Vista Grove Homes in Pasadena.

Grandpa and Grandma built their dream log home in Oregon. Jacci and Pat invited you and me to live next to them in Eagle Rock. This would be my new home for the next three to four years. I experienced new smells, new people, and new challenges. I never could resist chasing skunks. I missed Grandpa and Grandma and Powder Puff, but life went on.

Then one day out of the blue you sold me to the Cambodian lady and her eight-year-old son. My heart just broke in two; I felt very sad and missed you so much. Then about a week later, you, Jacci, Grandpa and Grandma came to visit me. I was thrilled to see you again. I remember it was a short visit. I was hoping you would take me with you when you left but that did not happen. But God did answer my prayer. I was overjoyed when the lady agreed to sell me back to you. I can't explain in words how happy I was to be with my family again.

Then you explained to me that I would no longer be living with you, but that my new home would be with Grandpa and Grandma in their new log home in Sisters, Oregon.

A couple of years after their log home was built, you came to live with us. It seemed like old times. All four of us had happy and memorable years living in Tollgate. I loved living there and playing in the back yard. I had freedom to run and play in a large area. I also loved lying on the deck in the sunshine. In the winter I liked lying on the hot floor tile in front of the log-burning stove. I passed my time away lying on top of the couch watching for cars that drove into the yard. I was a watch dog. I also enjoyed showing off the costumes you designed and Grandma sewed. I won first prize when you entered me in a PetSmart contest. I liked the way you dressed me up like a Pope one year.

You were my first love, Nathaniel, and will always be. I realized that Grandma needed special attention and love. She let me sit on her lap or beside her by the hour while she knitted. She loved me and I loved her. All four of us had happy and memorable years living in Tollgate.

I was sad to say good-bye to you when Grandpa and Grandma moved to Monte Vista Grove Homes in Pasadena, California and you stayed in Oregon. My life here at The Grove is much different than living in Tollgate. I have to be on a leash all the time. At Tollgate I could roam as I pleased, but, as you know, I did not go very far from the house. Here I have a bed on top of our old trunk so I can see who walks by on the street. Actually I do not miss the cold weather and snow we had in Central Oregon. It is warm the year around so I do not need to wear a coat when I go outside. Now my goal in life is to help make Grandpa happy because

Grandma is no longer able to live with us.

Grandpa tells me you will be home for Christmas and will arrive home on Christmas Eve. I look forward to seeing you again. I am excited!

This my life—my first fifteen and a half years anyway. I have had a great life and a wonderful family to be a part of. I look forward to having many more enjoyable years.

Merry Christmas, Nathaniel, and a Happy and Blessed New Year.
Love,
Felipe

- -

Not long after Felipe wrote his story, he began to have congestive heart failure and had to be put on medication. He stayed relatively healthy but his arthritis gradually worsened. During his last few months his health deteriorated. He began to lose weight and walked less and less. Finally, on December 10, 2014 at 6:15 pm, at Vanderhoof Veterinarian Hospital on Lake Avenue in Altadena, Felipe quietly took his last breath and passed on into the clouds of glory. He was cremated. His ashes, dog collar, and photo sit on a shelf in our living room.

Felipe

Howard Den Hartog

PLACES WE'VE BEEN

Gatsby's
Ken Grant

"How much did you say?" I asked. "Seven hundred fifty" he replied. I scratched my chin thoughtfully. "I'll put in a new timing chain too," he added. "She'll run just fine after that."

The object under discussion certainly was not much to look at: an old, rather tired looking and weathered convertible. The top was shredded, the upholstery tattered, the tires worn and the sun-bleached paint looked as though it had once been a shade of grey. But it was a Jaguar after all... and it ran! I bought it, new timing chain and all.

Over the next months I maxed out my two credit cards in a rescue of that old coupe. That meant a new, white top, "cotillion white" paint, new royal blue corduroy upholstery with matching vinyl trim and chrome spoke wheels discovered at a junk dealers. Of course that also required new floor matting (royal blue, of course) and new Michelin tires all around. Done? Not quite. I had the center section of the dash covered with a wood veneer like other "respectable" Jags I'd seen! The result was, I will admit, a rather impressive older car.

Now you must understand that this was during that portion of my life when I was single and without family responsibilities... or expenses. Now, happily remarried for these many years I look back with nostalgia, but no regret. After all, it did allow me to drive to Gatsby's in style. And that is a story that needs telling.

I was introduced to this elegant restaurant by fellow minister, Jim Froede, and his wife, Mary. Mary Froede was a very good pop singer and was then receiving coaching from Jack Latimer, one of Hollywood's top arrangers. Jack, as good fortune would have it, played piano at a decidedly elegant eatery known as Gatsby's located in Westwood.

Jim and Mary, probably at Jack's suggestion, would drive to the restaurant on Sunday evenings after the day's church responsibilities had been met and join Jack at the large, black grand piano that graced the corner of the impressive dining room. That room, with its white table cloths and sparkling settings was a thing to behold as were the tuxedoed waiters moving with subdued dignity across the beautifully carpeted floors to serve the obviously well-heeled clientele. Not to be missed was a long, massive and highly polished wooden bar that ran along one wall. Discrete, but part of a room whose every detail gave the impression undoubtedly desired: sheer elegance!

One day Jim said, "Ken, why don't you drive out and join us at Gatsby's this Sunday evening?" I did, of course, and I did so driving my restored pride and joy. The valet parked it right in front next to all the new Mercedes.

Mary and Jim introduced me to Tony, the manager who was also one of the owners. He greeted us warmly at the door and we were shown to a table next to the piano. Mary immediately introduced me to Jack who was her vocal coach. The Gatsby Adventure had begun.

I won't say I became a regular. It was a long a drive from South Pasadena to Westwood. And while I usually ordered a baked mozzarella with marinara sauce and a glass of red wine, the cost was not inconsequential after all. However, I did enjoy hearing Mary sing several sets with Jack accompanying. I was made to feel at home when Tony, on only my second visit, greeted me at the door with "Hi Ken! Good to see you again!" Yes, and the baked cheese with marinara sauce was delicious.

One visit, however, remains indelible. My Uncle Alex from Colorado came to visit. I felt close to him for he, who never married, had lived with us for several years when I was young. "Babe," as the family always called him, was intrigued with my tales of Gatsby's and especially the fact that motion picture stars were frequently among the customers. Some had, in fact, stopped at the table to compliment Mary on her singing to her awe and great delight! Naturally, Uncle Babe (Alex) and I went to Gatsby's that Sunday night!

I didn't order wine that evening but rather a Sambuca, a clear Italian liqueur on which they usually float a few coffee beans and which, lighted, is topped with a pale, blue flame as it is served. I'd had them before and so carefully passed my finger through the not very hot blue flame. My uncle, however, reaching over to do the same, tipped the glass, and suddenly my arm (luckily suited that evening) was a-flame with blue fire! Everyone gasped! I quickly grabbed my napkin and snuffed it out. Jack Latimer, at the piano, who had been playing something else, immediately modulated into an old favorite: "I Don't Want To Set The World On Fire." Of course, we all broke out laughing (Mary tells of this in her memories of Gatsby's).

Mary's memories also mention the many motion picture (and some Mafia) personnel who frequented the restaurant. While not witness to them all, by any means, I do recall Carroll O'Conner being there on my flaming night. On another evening I saw Danny Thomas and his daughter, Marlo, present with family. Another time it was the Gabor sisters, Zsa Zsa and Eva, at a nearby table. Tony and his sister and her husband, all owners, had clearly created a "going concern," Mafia or not.

But my story would not be quite complete if I didn't mention a simple and I suppose fleeting part of it all. It was the drive home in my beloved "XK 150". Top down or top up, the cool night air in my face, the old but still powerful Jag engine purring I cruised back along Santa Monica or Sunset eastward toward South Pasadena and my little rented bungalow on Huntington Drive.

There is one more memory to share and my last of Gatsby's. It was some time later and I had made a date with Caroline, the girl I was then dating. She had a dine-out card and we thought we might use it someplace. But where? Though undecided, we set out, ruling out this place and that and drove on... and on. Eventually we somehow ended up on the freeway headed west.

"Oh what the heck," I thought. "Why not?" The dine-out card would obviously not work, but then, Caroline had never been to a place like Gatsby's. So we drove on to Westwood. Though it was a bit early the restaurant was open and not yet crowded. We were seated by the usual dignified though friendly waiter and handed the huge menus. Ah yes! What to order.

I told Caroline to order anything she wished. She did, and the choice eventually was... lobster! I don't remember what I ordered, I just remember it was a delightful dinner. And the bill? I've forgotten. It didn't really matter either. I do know that Carolyn never forgot Gatsby's and that lobster, even though she later married a nearby neighbor in El Monte and they moved to Missouri to raise cattle.

As for me, I have my memories of an adventure with a wonderful old car that I rescued from a too early demise. Of course, I didn't use it for pastoral calls. I bought a used but respectable Volkswagen "bug" for that.

I do, however, thank God for those years and for friends like Mary and Jim. Jim is long gone now, but Mary and I still smile as we recall the unique circumstances that led us to this now long gone but fondly remembered night spot that was Gatsby's.

Challenges of Anthropology Fieldwork
Barbara Mathieu

To fulfill the requirement for a graduate degree in Anthropology, one is expected to do an original study based on fieldwork. For a socio-cultural anthropologist, it means you will be a participant/observer among the people you select for your research. The role of participant and observer requires walking a fine line between full immersion in the daily life of those you want to learn from, and retaining the objective lens of the observer—a difficult role to play.

I did my fieldwork in a rural colony of Hutterian Brethren, one of the three branches of the Anabaptist tradition—the other two being the Mennonites and Amish. Hutterites take literally the passage in the Book of Acts, "Apostles of Christ will hold all things in common." Unlike their Anabaptist (re-baptizers) cousins, Hutterites live a communitarian life in colonies with up to 150 persons.

It took me 18 months to find a Hutterian Brethren Colony willing to let an intrusive outsider move into their "intentionally separated from the world" community. Thanks to Joanne Hinch, who introduced me to Hutterites she'd met outside of Great Falls Montana in the early 80s, I was finally given access to a colony northwest of Spokane, WA. I had been in correspondence with the Senior Minister, Paul Gross, for 8 months when he said "Come on up to Spokane and we'll see about you doing your study here."

The day I arrived I had my suitcase in the car, but found I would not yet be staying. Instead, I would visit each household in the hierarchically structured community, presenting myself and my research intentions to each male head of household. I told them what I wished to do, why and how. Some asked me questions, others were too fatigued after a very long day in the fields, but then they had to give their okay or not to the Senior Minister. The women in the household listened intently but never said a word. A very clear division of labor exists between men and women, though I must say even though women did not have direct authority, they did have ways of asserting themselves and making their opinions known.

The next day I moved in to one family's home, that of Bill and Rachel Gross.

Hutterites eat communally, in silence, with women on one side of the dining room, men on the other. The men are served first and I could see whole roasted chickens, homemade noodles, fresh vegetables from the garden, fresh baked bread, milk from their dairy, etc. When the women were served, there were all the foods the men had, except we did not have roasted chicken, but chicken feet in a clear broth with noodles! Though the meal should be taken in silence, there was a whispering buzz among the women, and Rachel, my host-sister, leaned over to me to apologize for the Head Cook's choice of chicken feet for my first meal at the colony.

I knew then this was no "accidental" choice, but was a clear signal that though the men had given me permission, Margaret did not welcome me being there and made it known by serving the women chicken feet that evening.

I immediately whispered to Rachel that my mother was from rural Georgia and she'd raised my sister and me on chicken feet soup and it was a favorite of mine! The women at my table were quite surprised to see that I knew how to eat chicken feet as well as they did—just like a Hutterite!

After the meal, Rachel could hardly contain her eagerness to push me into the kitchen to tell Margaret how much I enjoyed the meal—and to let her know her message "unwelcoming" me had backfired! Margaret did blanch at my unrestrained delight over the meal, but it also broke the ice between us and we became friends!

Wednesday Afternoons
Gloria Shamblin

Uncle George and Auntie Doris had finally moved out and we had moved in over the shop. Although I had already helped in the shop, I had never been upstairs. What an adventure, so many hidden nooks and crannies. Everything was dark wood. I doubt that it had been painted since the turn of the century. At some stage my mother was to go in, paint, wallpaper, and change everything. In the meanwhile we had rickety banisters that went up very narrow stairs. These were replaced and the wall was soon covered with textured pink plaster which we combed into elaborate swirls whilst wet. All but the thinnest person complained when they grazed their arms once it was dry. No one ever got upstairs scratch free.

Upstairs there was a large living room with an open coal fire and a bay window that looked out onto the narrow one-way street. If you looked to the left you could see the Elephant and Castle pub sign. We shared a common wall with the pub, but It was so thick we could never hear anything through the wall

We had three bedrooms with high ceilings. Inside one of the bedrooms was a door about 3 feet high. When the door was opened there was a small drop that led into 2 long narrow rooms. A few years later the family would be sleeping here as my mother commandeered the other bedrooms to do Bed and Breakfast. My sister was to remind me many later years we called it The Dump because, to us, it was self-explanatory. It was a depository for old clothes and broken furniture to be repaired and then we forgot about it. But in the early 1950s they were just fun little rooms where we slept.

Downstairs behind the store was a small room where we did most of our living. It was heated by a solid fuel stove, a Rayburn, which was like the poor man's Aga. We had an armchair and a sofa and a gate-leg table which was not opened since there was not room. There, was also a massive radio gram, behind which there was one wall plug with lots of things plugged into it. I remember Mum's iron sparking when it was plugged in. Ironically, she was scared of lightning, always drew the curtains and we were not allowed to use our silverware in case lightning struck us through the window.

Beyond this room was a narrow kitchen with a very old fashioned sink and gas stove and behind this a long bathroom which contained just a bath. These long rooms had all originally been attached outbuildings when years before they had been stables and then a dairy. One room had a nonfunctional water pump. The one toilet was way down the end of the garden. It was a few years before a toilet was added to the bathroom.

When we moved in, the shop had not been changed since before WWI. The building dated back to the 1820s. The floor was wooden floorboards and the ceiling was painted with advertisements for sunlight soap and other grocery goods. I thought it was pretty. My mother was soon to paint that over with white paint to modernize it. In retrospect a lot of artistic history was lost.

There were steel-lined drawers in which we kept loose sugar and dried fruit. These goods were weighed on a large scale which we used for everything. After my sister was born over the shop, she was weighed monthly inside a cardboard box. Butters, margarines and lard were in big slabs on a marble counter; these had to be cut and weighed. The big round cheddar cheese was rolled in and was cut with a cheese wire. I became a whiz at this and could cut eight ounces of cheese by eye. All the fats were then wrapped in greaseproof paper; today it would be called parchment paper. We had a bacon-slicing machine with no guard and that is about the only thing I was not allowed to touch.

All deliveries were made through the front door as there was no back entrance; the back garden was enclosed by a high flint stone wall at the back. The deliveries were not large as rationing for groceries was to continue for a few more years. There were two kinds of soap in bars: washing soap and toilet soap. Not much choice between, probably the reason my mother never used soap on her face. It was before washing detergent and my mother kept boxes of soap flakes under the counter for women with babies only. She said they deserved soft things for the baby washing.

We had a big cash register which did not ring up the amount of money paid but the drawer would open and close. It was massive. Shillings and pence were very weighty in those days. There were a few pound notes and ten shilling notes, but it was a long time before I saw a five or ten pound note. We totaled up the prices of the grocery orders with pencil on paper and when they paid, we wrote "received with thanks" and signed our name. No one seemed to question a nine year-old working out change in pounds, shillings and pence long before the decimal system. Of course, one of my jobs was to cut, count and rubber band ration coupons. I wish I had some now or at least an old ration book. Apart from rationing there were all kinds of government laws regarding sale of groceries and perishable goods.

The one thing I loved about these laws was Half Day Early Closing. It was required that the shop would be closed Sundays and for half a day during the week. In Bognor this was Wednesdays. Mum and Dad would pick me up in the car after school. Somewhere along the line dad's motorcycle had disappeared so no more pillion rides for me. Sometimes we would shop in Chichester, their early closing was Thursdays. The stores were fancier there and sometimes we would look at some of the historic buildings. I always liked the ones called Georgian. In those days we could drive around the 15th century cross in the middle of town. We would usually get a cup of tea and a Chelsea or Bath bun. I loved the big sugar crystals on top. We had time to look at the Roman wall around town before we drove home.

Some days we would go to Batchmere. The Bowlers lived on a small holding. It was really a tiny farm where they kept chickens and goats and grew wonderful tomatoes in a green house. They supplied us with a very exotic fruit called a melon. I tried to avoid the usual cup of tea as goat milk gave it a horrible taste. We usually collected a tray of eggs and boxes of tomatoes that sold like hot cakes in our store. As we got to know them better, Mrs. Bowler would bring a freshly killed chicken which would share the back seat of the car with me. I did not enjoy a dead chicken which flapped her wings. When we got it home, Dad would hang it at the end of the garden and we would learn how to pluck the feathers without tearing the skin and singe the little pin feathers with a lit taper. I later realized I had a great biology lesson in the mysterious way chicken eggs are formed.

Other late afternoons we would go to the pictures in Littlehampton. I don't remember what we saw, probably a Jack Hawkins war movie or Fred Astaire. It was comforting to have my fairly new dad lift my sleepy body into the back of the car to go home.

If it was autumn, we would go blackberry picking somewhere in the country along the hedgerows and in the fields all free. We would laugh because always someone would step into a cow pancake. As time went on we would take a small Primus stove and kettle and make tea, maybe with fish paste sandwiches. Over the years mum became quite famous for her white linen table cloths which we always took on picnics often high on the South Downs. We would pass Goodwood Motor Raceway; I think years later we saw Sterling Moss. We also passed Goodwood horse racing. It was a few years before we saw the queen, wearing a headscarf.

Sometimes we would go scrumping, or at least Mum did. I was at Catholic school and Little Miss Perfect. Mum would climb over the hedge and gather windfalls into her skirt, and I was in dread a farmer might catch us. However, I had no guilt about eating a homemade blackberry and apple pie. I still like this tasty combination of fruits.

I believe these were maybe idyllic afternoons for my parents. The war was over, the country was free of oppression and they had a temporary break from their hard work. For me it was time with my parents before they became more consumed with another grocery store for holiday-makers, and, of course, the Bed and Breakfast.

JUST FOR FUN

You Can't Be Too Certain
Barbara Mathieu

In 1970, my husband, Jim was in his third year of graduate studies at USC. He was doing pulpit supply and part-time interims at various churches in the Southern California area. In the summer of 1970, a member of one of the churches who taught high school math spent his summers as a ranger in Olympia National Park in Washington State. He encouraged Jim to bring our family to visit this magnificent rainforest in the continental U.S. We drove to the Pacific Northwest, camping on the way with our three young sons.

Once there, he met us and invited us to have dinner with him and his family before bedding down at our tent-site. During dinner when Dan made suggestions as to what we should see and do during our visit, I told him I'd like to go on a mushroom foray—outside of National Park boundaries, of course—and he replied with a cautionary tale.

He told of his colleague and friend who, as the park's Naturalist, prided himself on being a knowledgeable mycologist—a fungi expert. He and his family would gather mushrooms several times a week for their family meals.

One particular evening, after an afternoon of mushroom collecting his wife was cleaning and preparing the bounty of mushrooms they'd harvested, feeding pieces to the family cat, who'd acquired an avid taste for mushrooms and who would pester his wife until she shared a fair amount with their feisty fungi eating feline!

Just as the family finished their meal of mushroom soup and sautéed onions and mushroom gravy on toast, the cat began to yowl and roll about on the floor. The naturalist, knowing the cat had eaten a lion's share of the same mushrooms they had just consumed, panicked! He loaded the four children and his wife into his station wagon and drove 60 miles to the nearest hospital to have their stomachs evacuated—a very unpleasant experience for all six of them.

Several hours later, quite wrung out from their ordeal, they returned home and found the cat had had kittens!

Our friend Dan warned that even the experts can doubt their expertise and suggested we open a can of spam for our camp toast!

A Stitch in Time
Mary Froede

I just returned from playing in a bridge tournament held in Las Vegas (fortunately, no money was involved). Of all the new people I met, one remains in my mind. Her name is Lucinda and she lives south of here (Pasadena, CA), almost to the Mexican border. I was initially fascinated by her beautiful turquoise jewelry, which I admired. She indicated that most of it was Navajo, and that the rings were "men's rings" as she was a rather large-boned woman. Her skin was a beautiful, tawny, smoky tan and her face, framed with grey hair pulled back into a type of pony tail, accented the strength of her face. She had high cheekbones, twinkling black eyes and a lovely smile. Her blouses always reflected an Indian theme, so after a couple of days seeing her throughout the tournament, I got up the nerve to ask her if she had any American Indian heritage. She was delighted to tell me that she was a certain percentage of Navajo, something I had already guessed. The most telling part of her story, aside from the jewelry, was that she was wearing a pair of glass-beaded earrings made up in the chandelier fashion. I was transported back in history to one of the favorite gifts I had received when I was about six years old. A bead weaving set. It was about twelve inches long and was threaded with the warp; my job was to add the weft which was about four inches wide. I spent hours making bead straps, bead bookmarks, bead do-dads that I presented to anyone who was willing to accept this weird gift.

Weaving waited until I was in college and joined an adult weaving class with my mother. We made some lovely runners, placemats, and napkins. I still had a few of them left in a later move after I married. When I lived in New Mexico, my fascination tended toward the back-strap looms where you sat on the floor, counterbalanced by hooking the end of your loom to a doorknob. I never did buy one, but probably wouldn't have had the time to do anything with it at that time as I was preoccupied with church activities and three children.

Crocheting never appealed to me, although, I can single chain forever, but then have to figure out how to make it into anything other than a lariat. Because I detested hand sewing and embroidery, knitting was my thing. My grandmother was from Germany and knitted the German way, which meant that my mother knitted that way as well. She picked up her yarn for each stitch with her left hand. In teaching my sister and I to knit, she sat across from us and we both ended up knitting the American way, by throwing the yarn with our right hand. My first ventures were just dishrags or small table cover pads, but by the time I was a teenager, I was really into the real stuff. I knitted a few sweaters for myself, and with World War II coming on, I knitted army vests for the USO. They were all khaki colored and couldn't have been more boring. At that time, I was an usher at the local theater, and after we seated people throughout the show, we could sit in the very back row and wait for our next customer. I learned to knit in the dark and was able to produce a good quantity of vests.

When I moved with my folks to Milwaukee, I was a sophomore in college and had a steady boyfriend. Argyle socks were the rage. I don't even know how many pairs I knitted, but they were all different colors and he said he enjoyed them. Well, his mother did not like me (he was an only child and spoiled rotten) so she took all the socks, made of wool, and boiled them!!! He said they wouldn't have fit a small child after that.

My next boyfriend was in the Navy. I was determined to knit him a civilian sweater for when he came home. The design covered most of the front and was the head of a deer with the antlers going over his shoulders to end up in the back. He was a pretty good-sized guy and so was the sweater. We eventually broke up before I finished the sweater and I ended up marrying my one and only husband, Jim. Naturally, he was the lucky recipient of the finished sweater. He was a good deal smaller and proceeded to drown in the lovely sweater. I turned it inside out and sewed it into a size that he could wear.

I still knit almost every evening. I am working on a lovely sweater now that uses bamboo yarn. Something quite new and different. I am anxious to see how the finished product turns out. With all the colors of scrap yarn that I have in my cedar chest, I also knit little caps with pom-poms for newborn babies. They are so cute and such fun to make.

The whole reason for this "essay" is to get to the point of the surgery I had last week. I had a basal cell carcinoma above my left eyebrow about the size of a nickel. I went in thinking I would be out of there in time to go the county fair with my daughter and grandson who was on leave from the Navy. Dr. Chang started operating at 10:00 A.M. with a procedure called MOH where they cut some of the growth and check it with a microscope to see if all the tumor has been removed. If not, they come back and start cutting again until they are sure they have it all. This was done three different times and I ended up with a hole one full inch in diameter and an overdose of Novacaine. I told Dr. Chang to quit when he got to my brain! I then had to wait until he finished seeing all his patients for him to put forty-seven stitches in my forehead. I looked like the widow of Frankenstein. I left their office at 7:00 P.M.

Ohhh... I meant to ask Dr. Chang if he had ever done any hemstitching.

Facing Satchel Paige on the Mound
Margy Wentz

My dad, Adolphus Grant Smith (1899–1990) grew up in Palco, Kansas in Rooks County. He was just over six feet tall and was athletic. He was first baseman on the Palco High School team. He also played on the Stockton High School team as one of his sisters was superintendent of school in Stockton. Palco also had a community baseball team that played during summer months after wheat harvest ended.

Leroy Robert "Satchel" Paige (1906-1982) grew up in the slums of Mobile, Alabama and at age 13 was committed to the Industrial School for Negro Children in Mount Meigs, Alabama, until the age of 18. During the more than five years he spent at the school, he developed his pitching skills. He began his professional career with the Chattanooga Black Lookouts, playing for a number of teams in the Negro Leagues, ending with the Kansas City Monarchs.

So how did two baseball players from different parts of the country, with very different backgrounds, and widely varied skills come to play in the same game? Enter two other elements of the story.

Nicodemus, Kansas is the oldest surviving town west of the Mississippi established by African Americans following the civil war. The unincorporated town still exists in Graham County Kansas (a county that is adjacent to Rooks County). The entire town is a national historic site. Founded in 1877 by some one hundred freed slaves, by the mid 1880's it was a prosperous town with two newspapers, three general stores, a school, bank, three churches and numerous homes. In the '50s our family planned our trips to Palco to, visit relatives and to have lunch at Ernestine's, renowned for its barbeque. The restaurant remained until the mid-90s, but Ernestine's niece Angela Bates still cooks in her home next to the Township Hall and does a huge take-out business of her ribs, fried chicken, potato salad and barbequed beans.

In addition to Nicodemus, the other great story is about the Kansas City Monarchs, a premier baseball team in the National Negro Leagues, and winner of the first Negro World Series in 1924. Just after the Civil War African Americans were allowed to play professional baseball, but Jim Crow

47

laws ended that. In 1920 Andrew "Rube" Foster, a respected team owner and former player called together several other club owners and the group formed the Negro National League, the first professional league for black players. One of the teams in the league was the Kansas City Monarchs. Jackie Robinson was playing for the Monarchs in 1945 when he was recruited by the Brooklyn Dodgers. Nearly every Negro player in the baseball Hall of Fame played at one time or another for the Monarchs, including Satchel Paige.

Well, now the cast is complete. Adolphus Smith, Satchel Paige, Nicodemus, and the Kansas City Monarchs. For years the town teams from Palco and Nicodemus played each other on the Fourth of July, followed by a huge barbeque and fireworks. For several years in a row Palco won. But that ended the year that Nicodemus recruited several of the Monarchs to play on their team. They continued to play for several years, enticed by the aura of Nicodemus and the aroma of the barbeque. And that's how my dad came to face Satchel Paige.

10,000 Steps a Day
Mas Hibino

I received an LG watch in October, 2014 as my 84th birthday gift from Larry and Lucy Page, my son-in-law Carl's brother and his wife in Palo Alto, California. I was very grateful for their generosity and thoughtfulness. After using the watch for several days, I realized that among many other great features, the watch recorded the steps I took every day. So I decided to walk 10,000 steps a day and record how many steps I took every day from November 13, 2014.

As I started to walk every day, I realized that my blood sugar level had come down significantly. I am a diabetic and inject insulin twice a day following my doctor's order. It is important for me to keep my blood sugar level down. This result encouraged me to continue to walk.

I used to drive to Lacy Park in San Marino from my retirement community and walk around the park three or four times and return home. But on Saturdays and Sundays, I was told that only the residents of San Marino could use the park. Since I am not a resident of San Marino, I started to walk around our community and our neighborhood on those days.

Then one day, I said to myself, "Why should I drive to Lacy Park and walk? It takes several minutes to drive there and several minutes to come back. Besides, there may not be a parking spot. If I walked within our community and neighborhood, I could walk from the moment I step outside." So I started to walk from my apartment to Rosemead Boulevard and back on San Pasqual Street. I was told that a round trip was two miles; it is about 6,500 steps. So I started to walk in my neighborhood. Of course, in order to make 10,000 steps for a day, I had to walk some more during the rest of each day.

From March 10 to April 10, 2015, I had a planned to go to Japan for one month to spend time with my youngest daughter, Emi, her husband, Sterling and their two daughters, Geneva and Elise, in Kunitachi City in Tokyo where they are missionaries. I also had invitations to speak in churches and there was a family reunion of my wife's family that always included me even after my wife passed away. I wondered if I could manage 10,000 steps daily during that trip. For instance, it takes ten to eleven hours to fly from Los Angeles to Tokyo. On the departure date, I had to be at the Los Angeles airport by 10:00 a.m. That meant that I had to leave my home by 8:30 a.m., and I would be arriving in Tokyo in the evening of the following day. So a few days before my departure date, I walked extra steps in consideration of the days when I could not put in 10,000 steps.

In Japan, it rains fairly regularly, so I made sure to take with me a light rain coat and a small umbrella. I took every opportunity to walk in the streets of Tokyo every day. Streets in Japan are safe, and I don't worry about someone mugging me even in the dark. So I was able to keep up my 10,000 steps a day plus more while in Japan.

From June 18 to 21, I was in Northern California visiting with my daughter, Barbara and her husband, Carl. They also had LG watches and were trying to walk 10,000 steps a day, so we walked together on the Stanford University Campus and in Dish Hills nearby, which is a popular place for Stanford people to walk. That day, (June 19) I walked 23,830 steps.

From June 22 to 29, I visited my good friend, Johnny Musso who owns houses in Hinsdale, Illinois and South Haven, Michigan. The Hinsdale neighborhood where Johnny lives is a beautiful area. There are huge houses and the yards that time of the year are just beautiful. Johnny's place in South Haven, Michigan, on the other hand, is among farmlands. Johnny joined me in an enjoyable walk. The only trouble I had was the many mosquitoes which constantly attacked us. I had to use mosquito repellant and swing my cap to drive the mosquitoes away. That part was not fun. I am so grateful that we live in the area where we hardly have any mosquitoes.

From October 12 to 19, Barbara and Carl took me to Rome, Italy to celebrate my 85th birthday. We walked a lot in Rome, and it was not difficult to walk 10,000 steps and more a day. Considering hours I had to spend in flight to Rome and back from Rome to San Francisco, we accumulated more steps beforehand.

As November 13, 2015 approached, I knew I would complete one year of walking. As I added up one year's walking, it came out to be 4,781,397 steps. That meant, I had only 218,603 steps to make 5,000,000 steps. So after 15 more days on November 27th, I did make over 5 million steps. Precisely I took 5,009,647 steps in 380 days (365 plus 15 more days). I divided 5,009,647 steps by 380 days, it came out to be 13,183 steps a day average.

I told my good friend, Arnold Ng, that in my daily walk I start from my house when it is still dark. He sent me a reflective running vest, which can be seen at night or during low light conditions. He was so kind to think of my safety because most of the time I wear dark clothes when I walk.

At this stage, I am planning to keep walking, possibly to the end of 2016, and hopefully make 10,000,000 steps. As I walk, sometimes, I sing "Just a Closer Walk with Thee" the author is unknown. This daily walk for me all started because I received an LG watch for my birthday. Thankfully there are other family and friends who also began to walk 10,000 steps a day.

"I am weak but Thou art strong.
Jesus, keep me from all wrong,
I'll be satisfied as long
As I walk, let me walk close to Thee.
Just a closer walk with Thee.
Grant it, Jesus, is my plea.
Daily walking close to Thee.
Let it be, dear Lord, let it be.

When my feeble life is o'er,
Time for me will be no more:
Guide me gently, safely o'er
To Thy kingdom shore, to Thy shore."

Only at Caltech
Judy Post

My years at California Institute of Technology in Pasadena were never boring. When people asked what my boss and I did, our answer was, "Whatever no one else wants to do." When professors wanted an appointment with him, he would say, "Talk to Judy; she's the one who tells me where to go."

I think my most unusual event started with a phone call from Public Relations. Four Egyptian generals wanted to meet with David, so I set up an appointment. While they were meeting with him, PR called again and asked if I would take them to lunch at the Athænum. The only professor who spoke Egyptian Arabic was out of town. They knew I spoke some Arabic, so I said I would be happy to. However, I could tell from their names that they were Muslims, and in their culture, a man is never seen in public with any woman who isn't his wife, and I was concerned that they would be insulted. PR called the Consulate and was told that these men had lived in France and England, and were comfortable with our customs.

PR made the reservations and gave me an account to use, so off we went. We were seated at a lovely table on the West Patio, and one of the men said something to me in Arabic. Fortunately, I knew the phrase, and was able to respond correctly. Another comment in Arabic, and the appropriate response, and they switched to English - I had passed! As we waited for our lunch the conversation turned to food. One of them asked if I had ever had Egyptian food. I started naming foods I had had, or cooked. One of the dishes surprised them because you will never find it on a Middle Eastern menu in America. We discussed the ingredients, and they were amazed that I knew about it. They were gracious and charming, and at the end of the meal invited me to Egypt. They gave me their cards, and told me to contact them when I got to Egypt and they would show me around. I can't imagine doing that, but it was a lovely offer.

As I was walking to lunch one day I stopped to chat with a professor, and noticed that he had a children's cartoon band aid on his finger. I asked him if it was one of his children's band aids. He turned red, scuffed his foot on the sidewalk, and replied, "I'm allergic to chalk dust." "Why don't you get a chalk holder," I asked. Totally serious, he answered, "Don't you think that's kind of nerdy?" "At Caltech?" I responded.

Every year a pair of Teal Mallard Ducks takes up residence by Throop Pond. The male takes very good care of his mate; letting her eat first, and always protecting her. I used to save bread from my lunch, and would feed it to them on the way back to my office. They began to recognize me, and would swim across the pond when they saw me. The male would hop up on the bank, stand at my feet, and put his head back, to have me drop the bread into his mouth. One day I was on my way to the pond and encountered a biology professor. He asked if I was on the way to lunch, and I told him I was going to the pond to see if we had ducklings. "Oh, is one of them pregnant?" he asked. "No, I replied, but they do lay eggs! Henry, you should know that! You're a biology professor!" He mumbled something about molecular biology, and hurried off with a very red face.

I told our Provost the story, and when he stopped laughing he said, "Now you're going to tell me who is it." I said, "No, I don't name names and tell tales, and I've already told the tale." Soon after I saw Dr. Baltimore, our President, and the youngest Nobel Laureate in history. When I told him the story, he looked disbelieving, then doubled over in laughter. A few days later I saw him in the hall and said, "So, Dr. B., have you seen any pregnant ducks lately?" He was laughing as he continued down the hall.

Another day at the pond, there were two beautiful white egrets fishing for koi. Dr. Baltimore walked up and said, "Oh, look, there's an adult and a young one." "No", I said, "that's a Great Egret and a Snowy Egret." "How do you tell the difference?" he asked. I explained the difference, and he smiled, and said, "You've just taught something to a Nobel Laureate in biology!"

The Ball
Judy Post

It was 1964, and I was the young wife of a Lt. j.g. in the U.S. Navy, stationed in San Diego on a guided missile frigate. The Cold War had the military on high alert, and there was a feeling that nuclear war could end the world as we knew it. President Kennedy had been assassinated just a few months before. The event was the annual Naval Officers' Ball at the Hotel Del Coronado. It was a diversion from the constant tension, for the officers, and their stay-at-home wives with small children. The excitement had been building for the wives, as we conferred with other wives to make sure we would be appropriately dressed in formal splendor to do our husbands proud.

I had made an appointment at a new hair salon to have my hair done for the evening. Since my hair is fine and silky I stressed that I needed someone who worked well with long, fine hair. I arrived on time, and a shampoo girl washed my hair, combed it out, and left me in the stylist's chair. Shortly afterward a woman walked over, lifted several strands of my hair, and said, "I can't work with this!" and walked off, leaving me sitting there with soaking wet hair. After I got over the shock, I marched out and drove home through tears of frustration, frantically trying to figure a way to salvage the disaster. Fortunately hairpieces were popular in the mid-60s. I dried my hair and secured a crown of braids over my pulled back hair. Hoop-skirted ball gown, long gloves, and a short cape completed my Plan B outfit, and off I went with my husband in his formal dress uniform.

The Prince of Wales Room at the Hotel Del is a large, luxurious ballroom that was once used to entertain a former Prince of Wales on his visit to Coronado. We found our assigned seats at a table for 12 with other young officers and wives from my husband's ship. After a while we noticed that it seemed that all the other tables had been served and people were enjoying their lobster dinners. Our soup and salad had been consumed and the plates removed from our table, but no entrees were in sight. Growing somewhat restive, one of the officers reached over to one of the elaborate floral arrangements that decorated our table, pinched off a small cluster of flowers and ate it. After our initial surprise, the rest of us began to snack on the surprising tasty offerings. Finally, two waiters came over with arms laden with plates, and we began to pass them around the table. Not the proper way of serving a formal dinner, but we were too hungry to argue. As the plates went around the table, one of the officers slid one into his lap, and took the next plate for himself. Another officer followed suit, and the perplexed waiters tried to figure out how they had come up short. Two more entrees were quickly brought from the kitchen, and we all began to eat. The two extra plates were divided between the members of the table, and we enjoyed our feast.

There was a lull between the meal and the beginning of the dancing, and I left the table with three other wives to seek the ladies room. As we exited the restroom, the U.S. Marine Corps. Color Guard was in place between us and the door to the ballroom. I stopped to give them time to march out and present the colors, but the Sergeant Major gestured for me and my friends to go ahead of them. Much to my horror, just as I stepped onto the ballroom floor, the trumpets sounded a fanfare, and the Color Guard fell in right behind us! Being a true Southern lady, there was nothing to do but lead the whole parade across a dance floor that suddenly seemed to be at least half a mile wide. I have never been more mortified in my life! All I could think of was how many ways I could kill that Sergeant Major!

I don't remember much of the rest of the evening. My husband was furious because he felt I had embarrassed him, even though I tried to tell him that I had been told to go ahead of the Colors. I'm convinced that the Sergeant Major did it on purpose, and got great enjoyment from having the Colors led by four very embarrassed young women, who wanted to sink through that beautiful hardwood dance floor.

The Yard and the Yardstick
Sherman Fung

Football. That was the game I followed in my mind's eye as the announcer described the action, play by play, over the radio (also known in those days as "receiver set"). This table model sat on top of a dark, mahogany-colored cabinet, which housed an RCA Victrola and a dozen or so records (78s). The cabinet stood in one corner of our parlor, right next to the sofa. Between these two pieces of furniture there was a space for the handle that a person had to crank in order to wind up the spring that powered the turntable. When I listened to the radio, my legs would dangle in that space as I sat on the armrest of the sofa. Saturdays and Sundays found me with my elbows propped on the cabinet and my ears glued to the cloth-covered speaker mounted behind the petal-shaped cutouts that perforated the front panel of the radio. Television was still about two decades off. Except for attending the games themselves, or viewing newsreel clippings in the movie houses, we experienced this spectator sport through mental images prompted by the running accounts that came through radio. The game engaged our imagination more then than today. Football was also a way of identifying with what we were not yet, but hoped to be -- someone deserving recognition from others.

Even in our San Francisco grammar school, we played the game -- in some form – as touch football. Instead of tackling the ball carrier, we only had to touch him with both hands to take him out. During my last two years of grade school I played the game after school almost every day during the football season. The adult world's interest in the game affected the time of year we took up the game. Football in the stadiums invariably ushered in our season of football in the school yard. This pattern did not follow the dynamics of our other pastimes. For some unknown reason, there was a season for yoyos, there was a season for tops, and there was a season for marbles. What made those seasons come and go, I never knew.

When classes let out around 3:00 p.m., we would all head for the upper schoolyard. We ran across the lower yard, dodging the lower grade children playing there, and with a spurt of energy galloped up the steps, leading to the upper yard. The asphalted surface here made running easier; also, there were no "little" kids getting in our way. A long eight-foot high wire fence separated these two yards. On the side of the yard opposite this fence stood a concrete wall that retained the soil underneath the neighboring Chinese Independent Baptist Church property. This wall, and the between-the-yards fence, formed the long sides of our playground. The half-a-city-block long yard provided enough length for a junior size football field. Washington Street bordered one short side of the yard. The opposite short side shared a property line with the Chinese Episcopal Mission. An even higher retaining wall of concrete kept the soil of that mission property from tumbling onto our schoolyard. Even that, however, could not keep water from sometimes washing dirt onto the asphalt. When setting up the goal posts, we didn't have to go that far back though.

For warm-ups we threw passes back and forth from a stationary position. The more experienced players tried running passes. Those of us who tried punts and drop kicks did not have to hold back our exertion. The yard had sufficient length to absorb our juvenile power.

Then came time to form the two teams. The two best players automatically became captains and alternately picked teammates from among us. All of us understood that the choices were made according to playing ability. Although I never was chosen first, at least I was not chosen last. Because of my relative beefy bulk, the captains valued me as a good line blocker. I couldn't play any of the back positions; I couldn't run fast enough for the end position. I could at least hold my own ground against attackers trying to get across the scrimmage line. Sometimes I got to play center. I tried my best to deliver the ball right into the hands of the receiver. That was hard to do with my head between my legs spread wide. I wasn't used to seeing things upside down.

Football then was more than a pastime for me. It was a revelation of who I was and what I wanted. I wanted to be part of the excitement that came through what the football game announcer described over the radio. I wanted the status of the upper schoolyard. I wanted the recognition of being chosen early in the process of team formation. I wanted to do well even though my world was turned upside down. How my fellow students regarded me in the yard told me something of who I was and how I was doing. You couldn't see it, but really the yardstick was there as much as the football was.

Toys
Laura Berthold Monteros

A couple weeks before my youngest son's birthday party—this was when he was about five or six—a friend of mine asked if it was OK to get him a cowboy gun for a present. Her daughter had her heart set on buying one for Alessandro. I decided it would be all right, though I had only allowed the kids to have squirt guns. I'm not sure why; I had a cowboy pistol when I was a kid and one of my favorite toys was a Daisy cork rifle I bought with my own money. On the big day, when it came time to open the gifts, there was a shiny chrome cowboy cap gun with fake pearl grips on the handle from his friend Lindsey. It was enough to make any kid's eyes sparkle.

I needn't have worried about Alessandro being transformed into a gun-toting vigilante by this silver pistol. He never played with it as a gun. Instead, it became a handy club with which to bean his elder brother. The barrel made a good handle, and the pearl stock packed quite a wallop.

Toys aren't always used for what they were intended. Duplos make great projectiles when one is angry at one's cousin, for instance. Barbies are a sex-education primer for little boys who get into their sister's dolls. Blocks are as much for knocking down as building up. Just about anything can become a club.

Each one of my children had enough stuffed animals for ten kids, and they did cuddle with them. The youngest, Gabriel and Alessandro, also played games that transformed them into tanks, space ships, and soldiers. I'm sure there were other creative uses to which they were put, like their bed pillows that became sumo wrestler tummies. Pillows have always been good for pillow fights, too, but I still laugh myself to tears when I think of the two battling it out with chest bumps on the patio when I told them to take it outside.

When my eldest son Carlos was little, his favorite toy was Box & Blocks, a red plastic box about five inches square with other boxes inside. There were two blue half-size rectangular blocks, two yellow quarter-size blocks, and two orange cylinders. The lid has a square hole and a round hole. It's recommended for 9 to 36 months, but he played with it long after that. I don't think he ever used it as a shape sorter; doing so would have been stifling to creativity. He made it into an imaginary friend by stacking the blocks in such a way to make legs, a body, and arms. He named it Dancy Dancy. More than 30 years later, only one piece is missing and I keep thinking it will turn up.

Some of the best toys aren't toys at all. I remember finding an old board that had been worn away in a rifle shape in my aunt's yard. I played with it when I visited and hid it before I went home, so my uncle's grandkids wouldn't find it and it wouldn't get tossed out. It was always in the same place when I returned. Sticks are good to use as swords or machetes or canes, and they can be used to tap rhythms or to smack one's cousin or sibling. My grandson Rafael's favorite toys are sticks and stones gathered from the yard.

A card table and blanket made a really neat hideout. I watched Mary Martin live on TV in *Peter Pan* from one of those tents. I could pretend to be in Never Never Land myself while I laid on my tummy in front of the television. When I became a parent, I made tents out of sheets draped between a bunk bed and the windows of Carlos' narrow bedroom. Later, he continued the practice for his younger brothers.

Kitchen items are useful, too. Pots and pans, wooden utensils, and in the case of Rafael, a French whisk that bounces like Tigger. Kids seem to like the real thing rather than toy cookware scaled to their hands. Of course, pretend cooking is only part of what they are used for, with the most common use being as musical instruments.

Real musical instruments are not toys, but they can be fun. The other day, I got out my French horn to entertain Rafael, who had refused to take a nap. In all the equipment that I dumped out to get to the rotor oil I needed, he found the bottom of a music stand, which he opened and carried around. He also came across a mouthpiece, a tuning fork, and a tiny statuette of a bear holding a horn. These were uncommon treasures; he clasped them in his hand and would simply not let go the rest of the afternoon. He did allow me to demonstrate the tuning fork, which was an epiphany. The A440 ringing so pure in his ear made the hunk of metal infinitely more valuable and clutch-worthy. He repeatedly hit it against the furniture and put it to his ear, but didn't quite get that the handle, not the fork, should go there.

When I was a child, my favorite superhero was Superman. There weren't many female superheroes at the time, so I liked to dress like Superman in a long-sleeved T-shirt in the proper shade of blue with the red and yellow "S" emblazoned on the front. An old towel made a perfect cape and rolled up socks stuffed up the sleeves became muscles. My big brother had a lot of fun at my expense over those socks.

Robin Hood was another one of my heroes, especially as played by Errol Flynn, though Richard Green's television version wasn't bad, either. One Halloween, my mother made me a Robin Hood costume and I rigged up a bow and arrows as I had done many times before. I used a kite crosspiece with string for the bow and cardboard arrows cut from the pieces of cardboard that cleaners used to put on hangers to keep from creasing pants.

Cardboard, especially appliance boxes, invite creativity, and when junk such as old plastic or metal items are added, one's entire world view can change. One summer, after saving a refrigerator box and countless items of valuable trash for months, the kids and I made a spaceship. I put an old poster of the planets in the front window so the kids could fly to the stars.

Nowadays, parents let their kids play with cell phones. Not just for the game apps, but as chew toys. When I protested, I was assured that online sources say that it's OK for a baby to put a cell phone in his mouth. I don't believe it and keep mine firmly in my pocket. There are some things that are *never* toys, however, which is hard to explain to toddlers. I have to remind my grandsons that they are to play the piano with hands only, not drumsticks, feet, knees, or hard rubber dinosaurs.

When I consider toys and things used as toys, I realize the value is not in the items themselves nor the educational properties assigned to them. It's in what the imagination does with them, the blossoming of creativity and the revelation of exploration. Mister Rogers said, "Play is often talked about as if it were a relief from serious learning. But for children, play is serious learning. Play is really the work of childhood." I wonder if maybe we grown-ups should work a little more.

The Life Cycle of a Couch
Anna Walker

When Glenn and I were married, we received the traditional crystal vases, stemware, and china that we have used only a handful of times in our 21 years together. We also received cash which was much more useful since we used it to make our 1st big purchase together… a couch, which I must add here, we used every day.

We spent hours looking at various styles and colors – too modern, too traditional, too uncomfortable – until we found the exact, perfect one. It was larger than most, with plush, rounded arms and deep cushions. And it was the perfect shade of ivory.

"Are you sure you want a white couch?" my mom asked when I told her.

"Why not?" I answered, "Ivory is neutral and goes with everything. I can change the whole look of my room by adding colorful pillows and throws."

"It will get very dirty," she said.

"That's what upholstery cleaner is for. Besides it's just the two of us, what could possibly happen." Famous last words from a young newlywed. About 4 months into our marriage, we found out.

Glenn had always had dogs in his family. Actually, it was almost a prerequisite for our marriage. Must want kids, must love dogs. Soon it became clear that, though we were not ready for children, we did want to hear the pitter-patter of little feet. So off we went to the humane society to look at pups. Glenn found a chocolate brown "lab mix" in one of the cages, looking so forlorn it almost made him cry. After a few days, this furry bundle of joy was ours. Casey *eventually* made a wonderful addition to our family. As a puppy, however, she was extremely stubborn and vindictive. She was also really cute and within the first week had made the house her own. She slept wherever she wanted, including the bed and the ivory couch. Upholstery cleaner did come in handy, and we used it often.

About a month after getting Casey, Glenn was out watering the plants in the front yard. When he came back in, he was shocked by what greeted him. The couch had been attacked; the fluffing from one seat cushion strewed across the living room. He really couldn't believe that much stuffing could come from a single couch cushion (no wonder the seats were so comfortable). He told me later it was the one time he actually thought about sending Casey back where she came from. Upon further inspection, however, he realized that she had not torn open the cushion as he had suspected. Instead, she had jumped up on the couch, somehow managed to unzip the cushion, and take the stuffing out. So she was smart too. We were going to have to watch this one. Glenn was able to put all the stuffing back in, but the cushion was never the same... always a bit lumpy on one side.

The years went by and the couch happily fulfilled its duty... mainly, we sat on it and sometimes put our feet up, the dirty dog slept on it, food got spilled on it... upholstery cleaner was still used, only now, it did not seem to do as good a job. We began to understand the wisdom in a darker colored couch. We went to a friend's house. She was about to be married. Everything was white; walls, carpet, and, of course, couch. Glenn and I looked at each other and smiled... yes, she would learn.

By the time our daughter Sophie was born, the couch had really seen better days. My mother-in-law was a very accomplished seamstress and had recently re-upholstered a chair and ottoman in their house. I asked her if she wanted to take on anything larger. She very willingly agreed to do so. We weren't sure how to uncover the couch so decided that the best course of action was to simply put new fabric over the old. So it was that our couch started a second, more colorful, life with a new, large print floral. It was happy again. The cushion, however, was still a bit lumpy on one side.

With a child in the house, the couch was proud to take on brand new duties. It was no longer used just for sleeping and sitting. Now jumping became involved. And running and jumping. And running and jumping and falling. We found out that cushions weren't the only places one could sit on the couch. There were arms and tops as well, tops especially, since that meant that one could see out the window. We just never knew... Also, more food, in quite the variety of colors, was spilled. Upholstery cleaner was still used, only now, it did not seem to do anything at all.

By the time Sophie was 5 or 6 years old, the couch was really in sad shape. Although structurally it was still perfect, the cover that my mother-in-law had made for it was now grimy and loose, and was wearing away in some places. A friend of ours owned an upholstery company in San Diego. We had had drapes made there as well as had a few chairs redone. We just never thought to send the couch as her place was so far away. I am actually not exactly sure how we got the behemoth to her, whether we rented some kind of trailer or were able to borrow someone's truck. In any event she was able to recover our couch in a solid burgundy chenille that was both stain and wear resistant. She also replaced both cushions so now we had no more lumps. She did a beautiful job and we felt like we had a new happy couch... again.

The couch had a new life and held up really well to all that was thrown at it. We had learned a little in our 12 years together... we now had covers for it, so the dog and the feet and the food would not be such a problem.

Casey got older and, as all good dogs do, passed away one warm summer day in July. Glenn held out as long as he could, but he was lost without a dog in his life so off to the shelter we went. My requirements were that the dog shouldn't shed much (that was my biggest "pet-peeve" with Casey), and should be no larger than 35 pounds when fully grown as our house was just not big enough for a Great Dane type dog. Glenn's criteria was that the dog must be female and must not be sick in any way. Knowing all this it should come as no surprise that we took home a male puppy with pneumonia who grew to be 85 pounds! But we weren't finished yet... we still didn't have our small dog, so, in what can only be described as a bout of temporary insanity, also got a rat terrier for Sophie for her 9th birthday.

You may be wondering what all this has to do with our couch. Well for starters... there was the hair. So much hair you can't imagine. It was everywhere, and especially on the couch. On the cushions, under the cushions, *inside* the cushions... it crept up and stuck in places I didn't think were possible... it could never be entirely vacuumed up. Then, there was the dirt. The dogs were active... oh so active. Our backyard couldn't take it. The grass ran away one day and left the dirt behind. The plants... they never had a chance! They were killed, one by one, torn apart or trampled to bits. And the dirt, seeking shelter, found its way in the house, all over my floors, yes, but also to the couch. Soon it became so bad that Glenn could hardly stand to be in the same room with the couch. No one wanted to sit on it. When I would clean it, the dust and debris would billow up from the fabric, shimmering in the sunlight coming from the window. I was unhappy, Glenn was unhappy, the couch was unhappy.

The couch had to go. I still loved the shape and the color, but a fabric couch was just not going to be an option anymore. We needed a leather type couch. We would have just reupholstered it again, but we really also needed more room for people to sit. So we put the couch on the curb, free to a good home. Within two hours, the couch was gone, we hadn't been home so we didn't know who took it. We welcomed our new couch home, a black leather type sectional large enough to accommodate a growing family of 5.

Later that week, while getting the mail, a car stopped in front of the house and a woman got out. She asked if we were the ones who had put the couch on the curb.

"Yes," I replied.

"I just wanted to come and say Thank you," she said.

It turned out that she ran a house north of ours for the mentally disabled. They had been in need of a couch and ours fit the bill perfectly. "We cleaned it all up and it looks great," she said. I was so pleased. Our couch would start a brand new life. It would fulfill its duties once more, it would be useful. It would be happy.

I was looking in an *Architectural Digest* the other day at a beautiful room all decorated in shades of white, off white and linen. The couch was an ivory color. For a moment I envied the owner of the room. But just for a moment...

OUT IN THE COUNTRY

From Goo to Jam - With a Little Help!
Pam Miller-Hessel

This tale is set in Bolinas, a small town of 200 if you count all the cats, dogs, and summer people!

"Splat!" A sticky, gooey mess covered the floor, stove and anything else within range. My anguish encompassed not only this immediate disaster and its consequences, but also the loss of a morning's work.

Earlier I had enjoyed the mild sunny morning as I gathered and picked plums from our large tree. The abundance of fruit meant jam for the winter as well as donations of bags-full to the rummage sale the next week. The tree shaded our lush garden of lettuce which we shared with the local gophers; I could nibble leaves as I gathered plums. It really was a beautiful day and I looked forward to a bike ride with my summer friend, Karen. Still thinking about the joy of that ride along quiet country roads, I went inside for the less pleasant chore of washing and pitting the plums. I had a large potful so there would be enough gleaming jars to satisfy my stepmother.

Finally, the hot purple sweet bubbled and popped. A quick test in a jar of water proved it was ready to gel. Karen arrived and I assured her I would be ready soon. Since it was such a heavy pot I asked my brother to lift it down to a lower counter for filling the jars. That is when it happened. Bart dropped the pot! The generous quantity of purple goo oozed and stuck everywhere. Fortunately none of us was burned. But gone was my lovely day, hopes of time in the sun. My spirit collapsed.

Before I could wail Bart and Karen jumped in. With three of us working the icky, sticky mess was cleaned up, not a spot left! Then we grabbed containers and headed for the plum tree. This time we just picked...no luxuriating in the setting. Back in the kitchen we cleaned and pitted plums, added sugar and pectin and put the pot back on. We more carefully moved the pot, filled the waiting jars and covered them with paraffin. Ahh, kitchen clean, everything put away, I grabbed my bike and away we went. What a beautiful afternoon!

Life Parades
Carole Bos

It has been said "All the world loves a parade." Why is that? Perhaps these demonstrations give us opportunities to dress up, hide behind masks, and show our "other self." Maybe we just love the thrill of drumbeats and drama. Other times parades are the most effective proof of military might or respect for leaders and special events. Ticker tape parades in large cities like New York or Chicago, now turned into confetti parades, give me a headache just thinking about the enormous cost and expenditure of energy in cleaning up a city! Excitement fills the air as people gather on curbs or behind windows over the parade route, waiting to hear the distant sound of music or approaching motorcycles or a stealth bomber.

My first memory of a parade was the annual Halloween parade in our small town in Michigan. For days we tried to envision an appropriate costume. For us three girls, it meant a visit to Aunt Ethel's attic. She saved everything and we were assured that some article of clothing or antique item would give us inspiration for a prize-winning outfit. My memory fails to recall any medals, but I do remember the laughter as we children marched down Fourth Avenue, our main street. Medals were not the point. Afterwards we bobbed for apples and relished the cider and doughnuts our town fathers provided. Our parents allowed another hour or two to "trick or treat" and although we threatened a trick if no treats were presented, only once do I remember soaping a window with wax because no one came to the door, nor did they leave a light burning. I'm sure I would have received a lecture from my parents if they had known—something about kindness and thoughtlessness and an apology most probably.

Lake Odessa, my home town, had two doctors: my dad and an elderly man who retired in 1950. He had for years had a limited practice. To honor his long service to the community, Dad organized a float, featuring two surgical scenes from 1900 and 1950. The 1900 end of the float featured a wooden table with a patient receiving ether being dropped onto a mask. The doctor was dressed in ordinary clothes and the whole scene looked much different from the one at the other end of the float which represented 1950. This surgical patient was on a padded gurney with two

67

doctors and a nurse with white masks and gowns. Tanks of oxygen and anesthetic were nearby. My sister Louise and my cousin Iola were the patients. The high school band played and community groups marched in this demonstration of love and support. Dr. Peabody, the retiree, loved the whole affair as he waved from a car provided by our local car dealer.

1958 found my husband Bob and me in Santa Ana, California where church friends saved front row seats on Colorado Boulevard in Pasadena where we could scrutinize each Rose Parade float, band and equestrian unit. Never had we seen such floral arrays nor creative interpretations of a theme. Part of the joy of this parade was the across-the-street banter of the crowd as we waited for the parade to begin. People came from across the world to view this spectacle and, of course, the Rose Bowl Game. Later, when we lived in Monterey Park for eight years, almost every New Year's Day, we would watch the parade for awhile on TV, then pile into the car and drive to the area close to the finish to see it up close. That was in the day when ladders were allowed and five-year-old Karen sat on the top with her dad holding her tightly. In the last several years we have viewed this marvelous community event from comfortable grandstands in front of Pasadena Presbyterian Church where we enjoyed a great breakfast and found the convenience of bathrooms close by. This is the granddaddy of all parades for many people.

When we moved to Westlake Village in 1968, all of our neighbors were new residents. Our street, Baronsgate Road, was the last street to be finished in First Neighborhood. We moved in February and slowly all of the 600 homes were bought by mainly young families. The first Fourth of July in our new community was to be celebrated the old-fashioned way! Every child who had a tricycle or bicycle decorated his or her bike. Almost every cul-de-sac of six to ten homes designed a simple, patriotic float. This alone developed camaraderie among virtual strangers. Every year afterward the celebration expanded. Karen and Steve, our children, once held the ends of a wooden dowel supporting the Liberty Bell which our family designed from a chicken-wire base covered with aluminum foil. A few years afterward we dressed Karen in a Betsy Ross outfit, complete with a flag on her lap, and Steve pulled her in his Red Rover wagon. He, too, was dressed in a colonial costume, but he was not too happy that he had to pull his sister who was three years his senior. He wore an almost British royalist sneer as he reached the end of the parade route. What fun we had as a family, thinking of what our entry could be! I wonder: Is there still such a parade in this special city, now 48 years old?

The Disneyland Parade has changed through the years—from featuring familiar figures like Minnie and Mickey Mouse, Snow White and Goofy to more sophisticated light productions of the same stories plus new movie heroes. One parade I remember is when Steve and Karen were in their early teens. We decided to stay through the evening and were excited over the parade's new light innovations. We had spent the entire day there and had found a wonderful spot along the parade route. I decided I had to visit the little girl's room before the parade. I ran across the parade route and when I returned to join my family, I was unable to cross the street because the parade had just begun. Have you ever witnessed an exciting parade all by yourself? I didn't know anyone around me. I couldn't turn to them and say, "Did you see Snow White's face? She's beautiful." or "Isn't that an awesome display of blue lights?" Watching a parade without your family around you is the "pits"!

When Bob retired in 1994, we took our time crossing the states between California and Michigan. It was April and we watched spring gradually unfold its beauty as we took the southern route and then traveled straight north to Madison, Wisconsin where we visited Dolores and Deane Hendricks. Then on we went to Holland, Michigan where we stayed in our cottage on Lake Michigan. Our goal was to paint most of the downstairs, but we had plenty of time to enjoy the events of Tulip Time, an annual event in the first days of May, commemorating the Dutch immigration and culture. We took in the first parade which included the famed Dutch dancers in provincial costumes and sabots as well as the washing of the streets. The second parade several days later included some of the classes from various schools. Bob and I found it humorous that many children who now lived in Holland were from Vietnam. They joined the forces of the 1860 Dutch immigrants in the parade for after all, they, too, were immigrants from the 1960's. Many Holland churches had sponsored Vietnamese immigrants during and after the Vietnam War and it was evidenced by this colorful parade. Asian faces atop a Dutch costume:

wonderful!

Wouldn't it be amazing to be on a parade committee? Who would be honored? How would we honor that person, group, or event? What act would merit a parade? Would the honor involve bands? Flowers? Floats? Costumes? Music? This question made me think of a trip we made into Los Angeles. We entered Our Lady of Angels Cathedral and found a seat and then began to absorb the magnificent yet simple beauty of the building. What my eyes focused on for a long time was the parade of Christians on the Flanders Tapestries from Belgium found on the north and south sides of the cathedral. Each tapestry panel depicted four or five individuals facing toward the chancel area where the cross is hung. Hebrews 12:1 assures us that we are surrounded by a cloud of witnesses who have gone before. Here they were, in silent procession, depicted by inspired weavers: Women, men, children, some figures with recognizable faces, some common ordinary people with no pedigree other than being a dedicated follower of Jesus, 135 saints and blesseds from around the world, 12 untitled figures of all ages and races, saints from the Renaissance intermingled with people from the 1st and 20th centuries.

In its own way, this became a parade for me; a parade of people who were called in a special way to become a "peculiar" people, people who invested their lives in response to God's call. In addition to these 135 individuals whom the artist John Nava designed, I began to imagine my own parade participants: people who were called to teach in Africa or Indonesia whose names I did not even know, people who had been put in my life to inspire, teach and lead. There was no band in this parade, no clapping, no fancy cars, no flowers—just my silent prayer of thanksgiving for this Communion of Saints, my cloud of witnesses.

The City Slicker
Martin Miller-Hessel

It was in the first year of the 20th century and Fortuna, California was a small rural farm town in Humboldt County. The three young men in farm garb could spot a city slicker from a mile away. The newly arrived young preacher from down San Francisco way was one for sure. With his starched white shirt, stiff collar and carefully knotted dark tie to go with his dark suit and polished shoes, he was a sure ringer. They were primed for him when he walked up to them and invited them to come to worship the next Sunday.

Their answer was the offer of a simple bargain: "We'll come if you can beat one of us at mowing a full row of this hay field" indicating the large field of ripe hay behind them. To their surprise, he accepted their dare then and there. Carefully taking off his coat, white shirt and tie, he set them aside and reached for one of the scythes. He was a young man of about 5'8" and trimly built. "This will be easy" the farm boys must have thought as the test began.

To their surprise, Charles finished his row before his challenger. Folk stood by their word in those days, especially country folk. So, the following Sunday, all three young men showed up for worship. I suspect they kept coming after that.

This story was enjoyed in our family, especially the way grandpa Charles Philip Hessel, told it: "I grew up working hard on my father's farms and orchards. I knew how to harvest even after college and seminary. But I'm sure glad those fellows didn't challenge me to scythe two rows of hay that day."

Not many years later Charles Hessel was called as pastor of Arcata Presbyterian Church farther north up the Redwood Highway. When Ford began producing its Motel T, Grandpa gave up his horse and buggy and bought an automobile for his wide ranging visitation and preaching in Presbyterian congregations without pastors. His Board of Elders granted him leave to go up to the Ford center in Portland, Oregon where he learned how to drive, maintain, and repair the car. His never lost his love of working with his hands, learned from his father, passed on to my father, and through Dad to me. I am worthless at auto mechanics but do love to tinker.

Country Life in Bolinas
Pam Miller-Hessel

In 1953 when my father and first step-mother told my twin brother and me about a planned move from bustling San Francisco, where we had run free since the age of eight, they spoke of a small town. Bolinas is north of the Golden Gate Bridge and over Mount Tamalpais on the coast. Special to this town was a tame young deer who roamed the streets. Sure enough Nita, owner of a coffee shop cum small grocery, had raised "Bambi" to greet people and give a special feeling to the town. I do not remember her having any family, so the deer may have been her comfort. Unfortunately, shortly after we moved in someone, perhaps the sheriff, decided a tame deer on the streets was a danger to itself and drivers. So away went the main attraction!

We moved in late winter so were quickly involved in the three-room school. Our classroom was the "big room" with fifth to eighth grades taught by the principal, who was usually a man working on his administrative credential or a masters' degree. As quick learners we benefited from lessons for the older students and by eighth grade a group of us were given advanced work to keep us out of mischief! In spite of that my brother, always looking for fun, did things like putting a snake into the plumber's daughter's desk during recess. Of course the class was pierced with a scream when the girl opened her desk! I doubt time after school and a mile's walk home prevented other antics. One joy for me was ringing the school bell in the morning. If my brother had missed the bus, I looked out the window and waited to see him close enough to make it. He must have flown the mile for he rarely missed the bell! There was a traditional old iron playground behind the school where the younger classes usually played. We, the big kids, used the rest of the yard for our games. A favorite was when Pinky, a year ahead of us, carried out the phonograph and enticed us to join him for square dancing. How we loved that! Asphalt under foot, blue skies overhead and known friends made for happy times!

Our group loved square dancing so much we would organize dances at the old Community Center on the Big Mesa. I do not know who supervised us or how we got that distance from town, but I remember the eeriness of the old timber building with stairs to balconies and probably bats overhead. At least once a small group of us arrived early and thoroughly frightened ourselves before an adult voice declared safety. We danced to records with the calls included. I think adults joined us for this small town entertainment.

In Bolinas, community was a high priority, or at least so it seemed to me as a kid. I suspect the isolation and small population enhanced the need to get together. There were the Presbyterian Church, the school and the Community Center for diverse gatherings. My memories of the old community center begin with eighth-grade graduation our first June there. The Big Room sang songs symbolic of our country's history. I loved it! Everyone came to graduation, a high point of the year, a celebration of the town's youth. Another time for gathering was the annual Town Meeting. The one I remember began with a potluck supper. I had baked two apple pies and delivered them to the kitchen. I heard a man ask his wife if there was any pie for dessert. When she said yes, that I had baked some, he responded, "I'm not eating pie made by a kid!" Well, he had a piece, or perhaps cadged a bite from his wife, and went back for more! Later, as the meeting began and gained heat in discussion, I realized I had the privilege of being at an old-fashioned form of government. Everyone had their say and whatever was decided was followed by action. I believe that was the meeting when it was decided to build a new community center in town and to move the fire truck from Duggan's garage into a proper station attached to the center.

Funded by annual rummage sales, lumber was purchased and everyday men of the town gathered to take the next small step toward a modern building. I was proud that my father, who worked late afternoon to midnight, was adding his bit to the endeavor. I know kids clambered up to walk the rafters and had other high jinks, but on the whole it was treated with respect in anticipation of exciting times upon its completion. And there was community fun… everything from card games to dances to movie nights. I suspect all 200 residents joined in something!

As a child, of course, I found other amusements. One of my friends, Elyse, lived on the Big Mesa at the RCA receiving station. We roamed the coast north of town, walked on cypress branches formed by the wind into platforms floating overhead! A valley on Judge Martinelli's property was our "secret" hideaway. One day we covered our swim-suited selves with mud and Spanish moss and proceeded to chase the cows. We knew we would be in deep trouble if caught since cows do not benefit from running! As far as I remember that was the worst of our adventures!

My friend Lynn, who lived in town, took care of horses for summer folk, so we had ready mounts to ride to the beach or up on the Little or Big Mesas. Most thrilling was the beach ride, especially when we turned back toward home. How they raced!! We had to slow them down as we turned onto the street or Mrs. Sharon, the grand dame of town, would be onto our parents. I loved horseback riding which, since we lacked saddles, we did bareback! We found an old English saddle in the Pepper's stable but neither of us favored it over the control of a bare back! Sometimes we would ride all the way out to Balzaan's dairy to herd the cows in for milking. I think the milkers' kids liked it because they got time off, but it really was not much of a job since the cows were eager to be relieved of their milk!

We also rode bikes all over the countryside. One time the boys were bragging about riding around the seven miles to Stinson Beach in record time, so we took them up on a bet. We would beat their time! I do not know how we thought we would do it. My bike was an old clunker with no gears! But off we went and we did it!! We beat their time!! However we were a bit scared as traffic whizzed by…nothing like today would be but when you are on a bike, anything whizzes by! What really surprised us was how quickly the story got around town! The wonders of a small town!

I treasure my memories and experiences in the country. I learned useful skills, and enjoyed kid-pranks. Community and working together became real and special values to me. This story does not even touch on the work involved to run a house and keep warm and clean, but that will be another story. This city girl adapted well to country life!

Friendship
Tom Wentz

Personally, I never had a pet as a close friend. Growing up, farm animals were utilitarian. The cat was a mouser, the dog was for community awareness, and chickens were for eggs, or, better yet, fried with mashed potatoes and sweet corn. We had ducks, cattle, and animals normally on a farm. Our renter's had a horse that I rode, but even the owner didn't consider the horse a friend. I belonged to the Cumberland County 4-H Dairy Club, and while in retrospect, I did acquire skillsets, the peer members were what were important to me at the time; they were my friends. In addition to these friends, I also remember I wanted to be a special friend with Frances Kreider.

4-H: Head, Hands, Heart, Health. If you live in town you normally joined the Boy or Girl Scouts. If you lived on the farm, you joined the 4-H club. 4-H is an association of friends with projects, who are learning life skills for a secular world. The four H's: I pledge my head to clearer thinking, heart to greater loyalty, hands to larger service, and health to better living...

My brother and I were in the 4-H dairy club and our projects were Guernsey heifers. My brother's calf was named Hope and my calf was Faith. Mother named the calves before they arrived and those were their names. Our 4-H club met monthly for fellowship and reporting on our projects. In between the meetings, we cared for our project: feeding, grooming, and training. Fitting and Showing were the criteria. Fitting was how one cared for the animal: groomed, feed, and the animal's overall good health. A little molasses in the feed did wonders with the calf's coat. I would rasp and sand the hooves and horns, curry the fur, and groom with clippers. Showing was more. It was training the animal to perform, both standing and walking, responding to your commands. The animal, with command through the strap attached to the halter, would respond by moving with proper gait, stopping with correct foot posture and attention. When I hummed softly, Faith would perk up her ears, a special effect. To me, it was akin to the Westminster Kennel Club at Madison Square Garden.

Boys & Girls Dairy Cattle Fitting and Showing Contest. August 15, 1952. Won by "Tommy Wentz"

One year, I won the County Fitting and Showing competition, the ultimate trophy for that year. I thought of my project as preparing for competing with my friends, rather than learning life skills. From the county competition, one went to the State Farm Show. I was a member of the Cumberland County dairy judging team. We competed and won the State Competition at Penn State University, and we represented Pennsylvania at the National 4-H Judging competition in Waterloo, Iowa. As I think back, I did learn about the four H's and my animal was also kind of a friend. As to the friendship with Francis Krieder, she married an Ashire farmer after high school, I moved on to college and new friendships.

In my teen years, having friends was very important. Belonging to the group of friends, having a girlfriend, and I think just being in relationship with those whom you trusted was critical to life experience. In many ways, 4-H friendships were an important passage of growing to be an adult.

Tom and Jerry
Norman E. Thomas

My Tom and Jerry were horses. Big horses! They may have been named after the clever mice in the Walt Disney cartoons. In my mind's eye, as a six-year old, they were as big as the Clydesdales in the later Budweiser beer commercials. And I got to ride one of them the summer of 1938. While my parents took a trip to Europe, Egypt and the Holy Land, my brother Don, age four, and I, age six, spent the summer with Grandpa and Grandma Thomas in Monroe, New Hampshire, where Grandpa George pastored two Methodist churches.

While Mother and Dad were having their photo op astride camels near the Sphinx and Great Pyramids of Egypt, I had mine in Monroe, New Hampshire astride Tom, farmer Emery's draft horse. It was probably a chestnut-colored Suffolk by breed. On him I looked smaller than a jockey on a race horse. Howard Emery was short and stocky. He tossed me above his head onto Tom and I grasped the leather harness and swung my right leg over the horse's broad back. With no saddle it was more a photo op than a horse ride.

That summer I got to experience the end of a farming era. For more than one hundred years the Emery family had farmed on rich soil along the Connecticut River using horse power. With draft horses, they had plowed, planted, tilled, and harvested corn, and sown, fertilized, cut, and gathered hay. Larger Monroe dairy farms already had replaced horse power with tractors. Mr. Emery, however, was 65 years old and had no sons. Upon his death his fields, very close to the town center, would be divided and sold as house lots for non-farming families.

A New Hampshire dairy farm had a silhouette like that of an Italian church. Instead of a bell tower or campanile, it had a conical silo used for storing silage--the harvested corn that became the fermented high-moisture winter food for the cattle. Instead of a sanctuary the farm had a high barn. Along the ridgepole at the top ran a rail and pulley used to hoist hay into the barn. The pole extended three or four feet outside on one end like a ship's prow. From it hay forks were lowered to pick up hay from the wagon, raise and carry it into the barn, and dump it in what was called a "hay mow". The horses provided the power that made this possible.

Alongside the barn were two low buildings—the milking shed and the family farmhouse.

I got to watch the summer phases of dairy farming. I observed Mr. Emery as he milked the cows by hand the way his father and grandfather had done before him. Progressive farmers in Monroe used milking machines. Howard petted each cow to calm it before setting his stool near the udder and in front of the back leg that, if raised, might upset the milk pail. First, he washed each teat before drawing the milk. They were as long as hot dogs. He squeezed and pulled each in turn down and the first "test" milk fell to the floor. The rest went into the milk pail—over a gallon from each cow both morning and night. Mr. Emery let me stand between his legs and wrap my small hand around a teat. It felt rubbery and warm, but I was not strong enough to squeeze it and pull down to get milk.

Me with Tom and Jerry

"Haying" was farmer Emery's main summer daytime task, to be followed by the spreading of manure on the fields once the hay had been taken to the barn. I watched as Tom and Jerry, outside the milking shed, waited patiently beside the pile of manure—a year's accumulation. Once the spreader was loaded, they pulled it back and forth across the fields. Inevitably, some manure dropped out onto the road as they passed. Yes, the pungent odor of manure filled our nostrils until an evening thunder shower cleared the air once again.

I have many happy memories of that summer of 1938. Monroe's population of 429 lived along a twenty-mile stretch of the Connecticut River, the boundary between the states of New Hampshire and Vermont. Few lived in the town for most were dairy farming families. But on Main Street, opposite the town library, was the church, the parsonage home of the pastor, our grandfather in 1938, and next door the barns of Mr. Emery, a dairy farmer. It was easy for my brother Don and me to go next door, see the cows being milked, feed the chickens, and pet the draft horses Tom and Jerry.

The parsonage (the name given to a Methodist pastor's house), like most farm houses, had a front door on the street that was rarely used, as did many Monroe houses. Visitors entered from the porch off the kitchen that faced south, the sunny side, especially in winter. There Grandma grew to profusion her English garden of rambling roses entwined on a trellis, hollyhocks, daisies, and marigolds. Across the driveway she grew vegetables. Nearer the maple trees she planted rhubarb that we enjoyed that summer in pies and on tapioca pudding. Fifty years later the rhubarb patch was still there.

Don and me...

Don and I slept in a second floor bedroom reached by climbing steep front stairs. For us it was like a hideaway place, with its small windows and low ceilings. With no upstairs bathroom, we used a Victorian-era ceramic chamber pot at night, with matching pitcher and wash basin. [Fifty years later I slept in the same room on a visit to preach at the church and share about my mission work in southern Africa. The chamber pot was long gone. In its place the pastor gave me a tin can to use at night. He was a former missionary to India, where they called the tin can a *gesunder*— what goes under the bed.]

That summer flew by. On warm days Grandpa brought out a shallow wading pool, while Grandma sprayed us with a hose as we ran around and splashed in the pool. Every Saturday we walked to the Town Hall where the church women prepared and served in the basement a baked bean and brown bread supper. Tuesdays and Saturdays were library days. It was well-stocked with books for children. On the Fourth of July Don and I rode the church float in the town's Fourth of July parade.

In 1938, we benefited from what was called a "rural free delivery" of mail. Each house, whether farmhouse or house in town, had a tubular metal mailbox on a post. The carrier delivered mail by car each day except Sunday. Those who had letters to be sent, raised a red metal flag on the side of the box to alert the postman of the pick-up. Don and I took turns that summer fetching the mail. Eagerly we awaited picture postcards from our parents. Through them we learned about the picturesque places they visited in their travels from France to Italy, Greece, Egypt, Palestine, the Balkans, Russia, Finland, Sweden, Denmark, The Netherlands and England. Grandpa bought Don and me small notebooks for our beginning stamp collections. We wrote the names of each country on a separate page and pasted stamps received. He also bought us some stamps in packets to augment our little collections. That was a beginning of a hobby that continued to stimulate my interest in geography and world history in the years that followed.

At the end of summer Mother and Dad returned from their eight-week trip. After hugs and kisses, we opened presents. It was like Christmas. Then we shared about our happy adventures that summer with Grandpa and Grandma. "What did you enjoy the most?" they asked Don and me. And we replied: "The rides on Tom and Jerry."

SEASONS

Autumn Memories
Carole Bos

Those of the Midwest who look forward to the change of weather from season to season often allege they could never live in California where the weather is always the same: sunny with fair skies. My usual retort is that we do have a very real spring here, not with tulips, forsythia, trilliums and violets necessarily, but our world bursts forth with azaleas, camellias and blankets of desert lupine and poppies in splendid beauty. Our winter attracts "snowbirds" from the north escaping sleet, ice, snow and freezing temperatures thus proving we have a real advantage when it comes to winter comfort. If we want snow, we need only drive to the nearby mountains. Summer has seemed endless lately, especially in the last few years when temperatures soared in triple digits and rain became a scarce commodity. We surely have attempted to accommodate the demands of climate change.

I must admit, however, that I miss the Midwestern autumn of my youth when the world turned into a fantasy of complementary colors. Maple, oak, and sycamore trees furnished reds and yellows to canopy the streets. In the marshier areas sumac turned magically into plumes of fire. I remember the rich palette of color which was especially beautiful when traveling along stretches of rural back roads through hills and valleys. Vast acres of trees and bushes suddenly appeared, providing brilliant scarlet, crimson and yellow in the distance. Emerson called it "God's handwriting."

There was a certain smell to autumn. Cooler temperatures offered a welcome greeting. Morning dew provided a certain rich, loamy odor. Gradually the world looked and felt different. Breezes encouraged leaf decoration on every available space. We often selected certain shapes and colors, ironed them between waxed paper thus preserving the leaves for several months for use in table and window trimming.

Mother Nature fulfilled her promise of abundance. Grapes were ready for jam-making; isolated corn stalks stood like sentinels in empty fields. Nuts, cones and pods scattered over lawns and farm acres, thus investing in future treasures. Beginning their winter storage, squirrels scampered endlessly between lawn and secret depositories. How wondrous their preparation for long, cold months! This truly was a season of gift-giving. Our generous gardens gave us gourds, squash and pumpkins. As we roamed the woods, we felt blessed indeed if we found sprigs of bittersweet hiding among other brambles. What better decoration for a fall table than small pumpkins, gourds, and pieces of bright orange bittersweet, their flowers like popped corn?

Fall also had its own tastes. I love a summer pie made with rhubarb but my favorite autumn taste is pumpkin with its cinnamon, nutmeg and ginger flavors. Pumpkin was infused into bread, pie, soup, muffins and even into ice cream. The added kitchen aroma of seeds in the oven baking slowly made us impatient to crack them open and enjoy the salty treat. At one time we had an old apple orchard on our acreage. The trees produced only small, often bruised apples, but we gratefully gathered them and took bushels to the cider mill for harvest enjoyment through the winter months.

We three girls, ordinarily shirking the duty of sweeping or raking leaves, never minded the autumnal duty of gathering them so that we could jump into the magical, dusty tower of color in celebration of a fall ritual. Afterwards we raked them to the street, lighting them for a glorious marshmallow roast in the days when that was still legal. Burning leaves have such a nostalgic odor.

Mostly, autumn was a prismatic transition between leisurely, summer days and the beautiful but rigorous season of winter which demanded endurance and an appreciation for the demands of life. Always, there were the colors to remember: I have only to close my eyes to see, smell and taste this special season of the year.

A Little Shook Up
Sherman Fung

Our Thanksgiving celebration in 2015 was again with family. We were invited to the home of a family in Encino for a mid-afternoon dinner. We were guests of this same family last year, so this year we expected the guests who were familiar to us. We also knew, nevertheless, that we would be doing a lot of catching up -- babies added to families, addresses and telephone numbers of those who had moved or change of jobs, new hobbies and interests undertaken. Renewing contacts may mean patiently listening to long tales of happenings like the contents of some Christmas newsletters. We were not surprised, however, to find some guests there whom we did not know, so we spent a lot of our energy telling them about ourselves and getting them to acquaint us with their identity.

We had arrived at the party around 4:00p.m. By 10:00 p.m. all this adult gabbing and the noise of young children, yelling and running around, saturated our nervous systems. We were ready for home and bed. Our son Ken mercifully sensed our need and drove us to his house for an overnight stay. He fixed a place for us to sleep in his office, a small room that had a daybed squeezed into half of its space. The bed had a trundle feature. From the bottom section of the daybed, he pulled out a long box with an open top. Inside, the box contained a wood slat frame that served as springs. From the daybed he removed one of the mattresses and placed it over that frame. Now the two mattresses became an even platform. Because the room space was now even tighter than before, it was necessary for us to sleep across the two mattresses rather than each of us on the length of a separate mattress.

The house was very quiet since Ken's children were still out with Talin, their mother, at the party. Soon Alyse and I fell asleep. Not too far along into the night a loud bang startled us awake. My eyes opened onto the hardly visible shapes of the ceiling. My body felt funny; was I lying down or was I sitting up? Actually my upper torso felt half upright; my legs felt as if they were draping over something; my butt was resting on not the warm mattress, but something cold and hard. I was leaning sideways toward the center of the bed as if the center of that day bed had transformed itself into a shallow spout in order to channel us to the floor. Alyse was as bewildered as I was.

The noise, of course, quickly brought Ken and Talin (who by now had returned from the party) into the room. Surveying the chaos, they exclaimed, "What happened? Are you hurt?" They helped us get unraveled. The ambient light from the hall way immediately revealed that our bed had collapsed. An earthquake hadn't jolted us out of bed; a mudslide hadn't pushed the house off of its foundation; we hadn't been trampolining the bed; we hadn't been doing gymnastics; we hadn't been Greco-Roman grappling or Sumo lifting and pushing on the mat. We were just trying to get our Z's. What led to the separation of the two bed parts? Could all those appetizers, chips, candy, lemonade, turkey, chicken, ham, stuffing, gravy, sweet potatoes, Persian rice, salad, side dishes, cake, ice cream, and latte coffee immediately added weight on us that the bed couldn't hold up?

Whatever the cause, even though our systems were rudely shocked, fortunately no bones were broken. Not even a scratch, only a little shaken by the realization of how helpless we are sometimes. It is then advisable on future overnight stays to ask our host to help check on the security of the bed we are to sleep in, lest a trundle becomes a tunnel to disaster.

The Christmas Goat
Bruce Calkins

We had four goats, but only Tootsie was a Christmas goat. The others were named Bambi, Moose, and Scape. (Scape was Tootsie's son.)

I tried to train Bambi to pull a sled in the snow so he could be a Christmas goat. It was easy enough to dangle a carrot from a long bamboo pole, but fashioning a harness out of clothesline rope was a daunting task. However, the harness didn't matter. Bambi ignored the carrot and hopped onto a snow bank. The sled came to a sudden stop. This happened on every try (either Bambi or I was a slow learner). Bambi smelled like the billy goat that he was. He's the [expletive deleted] goat that ate all one hundred chrysanthemums that my wife, Lynda, had planted. The baby Jesus might have smiled at Bambi, but it took more than that to qualify as a Christmas goat.

The honor of being a "Christmas goat" went to Tootsie, our first goat. As our son, Wesley, approached his tenth birthday he had only one request; a goat. Wes took good care of our dogs and cats. He would sing to them. He wouldn't sing for people, but he sang to his animals.

A Christmas goat?

None of us knew anything about buying or caring for a goat. We had to learn fast. A few miles away, there was a farmers' market and auction. They auctioned cars, plants, 100-pound bags of potatoes, and animals. On the Saturday before Wes' birthday, I went to the auction. I had two responsibilities: to learn how an animal auction worked and to come home with a goat. I watched them auction dogs, cats, chickens, and turkeys. The prices were reasonable, but what would a goat cost? Which goat would make the best pet? Which one liked music?

They started bidding on the goats. They were selling in the $25 to $40 range. I watched until they got to the last goat, a young kid. I didn't have time to learn anything more. No matter how the bidding went, I *had* to come home with that goat. For $35 Wes had a birthday gift of a female Angora kid. He would have an audience for his songs. Tootsie was a winner; however, she was not yet a Christmas goat.

Tootsie must have known that to become a Christmas goat she'd have to go caroling door to door. Since *we* hadn't offered her this choice, she decided to venture forth on her own.

We kept all our goats on chains with clips at the end, but goats twist around a lot, and it's not uncommon for them to escape. Tootsie was more than a year old the night she escaped and went Christmas caroling. Our neighbor across the street was getting home from her 3:00 to 11:00 p.m. shift as a nurse. As she started to open her front door, she heard a goat in her bushes, "baaa." She wasn't sure what to do about this. She opened the door and went in. Tootsie followed. Perhaps Tootsie thought that, like other carolers, she was being invited in for hot chocolate. Our neighbor went upstairs to tell her husband there a goat in the house. Tootsie followed. When her husband woke up, Tootsie was standing on his chest. We never heard what his exact words were, but his wife brought Tootsie back to our house. Tootsie hadn't yet qualified as a Christmas goat, but it wasn't for lack of trying.

One winter night, the temperature dropped to zero. Wes brought the goats into the cellar. We barricaded the kitchen door so the goats couldn't get into the living quarters. But a barricaded door was no match for Tootsie. When we came downstairs the next morning, there was Tootsie, eating a potted plant. It was her Christmas snack.

Tootsie's inauguration as a Christmas goat came as a result of an act of generosity by Lynda, combined with her love of classical Christmas music. About 1978, Lynda was listening to the local news on the radio as she prepared crusts for seven Thanksgiving pies. One news item aroused her indignation. Because of reduced funding, the senior centers in Philadelphia would be closed on Thanksgiving. Lynda laid down her rolling pin, picked up the phone, and called the radio station.

Those were the days when human beings answered phones. Lynda was referred to a news editor. She repeated the news item about the closings and asked, "What are you going to do about this?"

The editor said, "What do you mean?"

Lynda said, "We have enough food, and we can fit six people in our station wagon. Give us the name of one of these centers and we'll pick up six seniors for Thanksgiving dinner. I bet there are lots of others who can do the same thing."

The editor took Lynda's name and number. Soon a reporter called and interviewed her on air. The reporter gave the number folks could call to make contact with seniors and invite them to dinner. Lynda was right about having enough food. She always had a 26 lb. turkey and seven pies, no matter how many were coming to dinner. My job was to drive into Philadelphia and fill up the station wagon.

After the meal, our family and six guests were sitting around getting acquainted. Lynda and I had a brief meeting. We agreed that we couldn't invite our new friends to just one meal. Christmas was coming soon. So, before we started back to Philadelphia we invited them all to come on Christmas Day for another one of Lynda's special dinners.

It was at that next Christmas that Tootsie achieved her status as the Christmas goat. Angora goats are white and fluffy. They look a lot like a lamb that has just had a perm. We moved Tootsie close to the front door, tied a red bow around her neck, and posted a sign with a line from one of Bach's cantatas, "Where sheep may safely graze."

For the next eight years, every Thanksgiving and Christmas, I picked up our friends. Lynda cooked a 26 lb. turkey and seven pies. And every Christmas Tootsie was by the front door, safely grazing.

Christmas Gifts!
Judy Post

There is an old English tradition that guests at Christmas are greeted at the door with the exclamation, "Christmas gifts! Christmas gifts!" The one who utters the greeting first gets to open his or her gifts first.

The frost on the red dirt road crackled under our tires as the car traveled between the snow banks on the sides of the road. The trees in the forest were mounded with snow, and it lay in a thick, undisturbed blanket under the trees. We coasted slowly into the driveway of a small farmhouse set off by itself, near the forest. The snow crunched under the tires, as Daddy quietly turned off the engine. Silently, Mother, Daddy and I slipped out of the car, gathered our gifts, and gently pushed the doors closed. Walking as softly as possible, we made our way up to the house, but just as we reached the steps, the front door would be flung open, and the joyous Old English greeting of, "Christmas Gifts! Christmas Gifts!" would ring out over the frosty fields, in the gathering twilight. We bounded up the steps to embrace my uncle, and be ushered into the house, where a roaring fire invited us to shake off the winter chill and settle in to wait for other relatives to arrive.

Soon children of all ages were racing and tumbling around, while the men lined up in front of the fireplace talking farming or politics. Somehow they all seemed to respond to an unheard signal to turn in unison to toast their backs, and later, their fronts again. Women gathered in the kitchen to help with the last minute dinner preparations, and to share information about the neighbors - who was ill, and who was improving, who had just had a baby, or gotten engaged.

When my aunt called everyone to dinner, the adults stood behind their chairs at the big table, while the children gathered around a smaller table with child-size chairs. After the blessing was pronounced, the men held the ladies' chairs for them to sit first. Daddy always seated me after he had seated Mother, even when I was at the children's table. The adults' table was a "groaning board," with ham from the farm, turkey shot by my uncle, and a venison roast contributed by an uncle or cousin. Vegetables canned or frozen from the garden, mashed potatoes, freshly churned butter, and home-made rolls fought for space on the table. The children were served from the larger table, and were closely watched for signs of mischief or misbehavior. Fruitcake baked in the old wood stove, my aunt's special custard ice cream, and a congealed salad were offered for dessert, along with other delights, while everyone protested that they couldn't eat another bite; well, maybe just a tiny sliver of fruitcake, and a small scoop of that ice cream.

After dinner, the board wasn't groaning, but we were as we moved back into the living room, with the men ranged again in front of the fire. At last the gifts were distributed to the excited kids, and the adults, who pretended not to be excited about it all. Soon there was wrapping paper and ribbon scattered everywhere, and adults and children alike were showing off their new treasures. My uncle would go to the front door to look out, and would turn with his eyes sparkling, and announce in a hushed voice, "It's snowing!"

My memories of those long-ago Christmases have been burnished to a fine sheen by the years that have past. The aunts and uncles, and some of the cousins are gone now, peacefully asleep down the road in the little country churchyard, the road has been paved, the farm has been sold, the house is gone, and those of us left behind are passing on the memories to the next generation, that they may understand that the love and closeness of family are a precious gift, second only to the most precious gift of all - the Baby whose birth we celebrate on Christmas Day.

The Meaning of Christmas
Judy Post

When I was about fifteen, my church began having a Living Nativity on the three nights before Christmas. A shed was built, a donkey procured, a hay bale put out, and people signed up for the part they wanted on their preferred night. There were five alternating half-hour shifts each night. I always signed up to play Mary on Christmas Eve. Most of the cast was from our youth group. Sitting or standing without moving for half an hour is not easy to do. I had a small three-legged stool to sit on but there was no cushion on that little wooden stool. We wore heavy clothes under the costumes, for the nights were cold and crystal clear. Thousands of stars spread across that blue-black sky. Christmas carols played in the background, and we were aware of the people who came to view the scene.

Hoping to make the time go faster, I began to meditate on what it must have been like for Mary on that incredible night. Here was a young, uneducated, peasant girl from a small village who was about to deliver a baby in a cave surrounded by cattle on a cold winter night. Her husband was having trouble believing her story of seeing an angel and being pregnant by the Holy Spirit. Really? Even so, he was protective of her and cared for her as best he could.

Mary must have been apprehensive about what she was facing, even though she believed what the angel had said. The cave might have been lit by the magnificent star that appeared overhead. As tired as she must have been after the birth, she would have rejoiced that her baby was safely born. Did she understand the life he would live and the death he would endure for a sinful world? It probably seemed unreal when suddenly shepherds appeared, telling of angels talking and singing to them.

At the end of each half-hour shift we went back into the education building to warm up and sip hot chocolate. After getting warm, we went back out for our second shift. Again I tried to imagine what Mary might have felt. It wasn't easy to do. Mary's life was so different from mine, but I called up everything I had read in the Gospels to help me understand.

After our third shift we changed from our costumes to street clothes, drank some more hot chocolate, and walked across the lawn to our chapel that was lit only by candles. The solemn and beautiful Christmas Eve service celebrated the birth of the Christ Child once more. Throughout the service the organ played carols softly in the background. At the end of the service we silently filed out of the chapel. It was Christmas Day, and some people whispered "Merry Christmas" as they hugged friends, but many of us went silently to our cars, deeply moved by the what we had experienced.

I played Mary for five years, and my faith increased each year. The sixth year there was a Christmas pageant in the sanctuary. I had married the previous summer and moved away from Richmond. I was surprised when someone called and asked if I would play Mary in the pageant. I was honored that they had chosen me. The following year my daughter was born on Christmas Eve morning. The church bulletin announced my daughter's birth and added "Judy played Mary in the Christmas pageant once too often."

Grandmother's Story: The Great Blizzard
Pam Miller-Hessel

As a child I loved my grandmother's stories of her childhood. One that especially caught me was the one of her family's journey out to their homestead. The version I knew until very recently was this.

Great-grandfather Walt Hardison heard of some wonderful land in Eastern Washington. After traveling to view it he decided the house and outbuildings would be fine for immediate residency. He decided to homestead it using his eldest son's homestead right. His family was living in Oregon on Yaquina Bay, a site with wonderful weather but not able to support a family with agriculture. He got his family as far as Portland where he filed the claim to his family's future farm and home. Then he loaded his family in a wagon and began the trip. Weather was cold but fine for travel when they set out, but soon a blizzard began. Great-grandfather bundled his family in the back of the cart to keep them as warm as possible and went on. Of course, the road soon proved impassable and there was no civilization in sight. Fortunately out of this blur arose a group of Indians, probably of the Klickatat Tribe, who gathered them up and took them to their village. The family was soon warm, fed and safe. Great-grandfather lost a toe or finger from frost bite but the rest of the family was unharmed. When the weather cleared they helped Great-grandfather go on to his homestead.

Not only did this give us a warm feeling about the Native Americans, but added to that was the news that Walt Hardison forever allowed the tribe to camp on his land to gather whatever they needed there. Grandma grew up playing with the children and knowing their language. Obviously the relationship was mutual.

My understanding was that Grandma was not yet born, but she and her younger brother, Wesley, were born out on the homestead. Certainly her stories of wonderful play, reading and exploration during childhood only included Wesley and the homestead. She loved this land and books. That was the message!

Recently I tackled a family file box. Included was an old binder with family stories by my grandmother. It was too thick to read at once so

I skimmed parts until I came upon this story of travel to the homestead. It seems odd that Grandma would have written this variation on her original story, but here it is:

Both Grandmother and her brother, Wesley, were small children when the family moved to Eastern Washington from Yaquina Bay, Oregon. Her father had traded for the land and then discovered the man, Jess Watson, had no legal right to it. Mr. Watson had added some fencing and a house, but it was really government land! Anyone could go and settle it with a claim. Fearful of that happening, Walt Hardison hurried his family to move in winter. They took trains to Portland and then on to The Dalles where they stayed in a hotel for the night. In the morning, Walt tried to find a conveyance to carry his family across the Columbia and over the mountain to the homestead. No one wanted to send a team of horses out in potentially snowy weather, but finally one man said his son could take them in a hack, an open vehicle. They quickly crowded in and set out. Everything went all right although the family, without warm winter clothes, was very cold from the outset. However, as they began to climb the mountain the light snow developed into a blizzard. Unable to see ahead or plow through the snow they were forced to stop. The men tried to dig out the wagon as Grandma's mother walked the two youngest in an attempt to warm up. They had just climbed back into the hack when a very large Indian astride a big black stallion appeared. He told them to find shelter at the nearest farm. When my Great-grandfather refused, the man said, "The papooses are all memelose! Look your hands are frozen now, old man! Go back to the farm house."

They did as told and the Indian went with them to introduce them to that family. The Gilmores readily opened their home and took care of everyone. Great Grandfather's hands needed special care as they thawed and returned to some state of function. The young children were ill from exposure for quite a while. But they were in good hands. In fact, not only did the Gilmores care for the Hardisons through a second blizzard, but when the Hardisons left two weeks later they also sent food enough to last until the family could fend for itself. Thus we learn of the mutual care of pioneers!

My Great-grandfather's hands were frozen stiff after that dauntless ride. Through the rest of his life his hands were disabled as though burned. There were some things he never could do. Fortunately, he had a couple of grown sons and daughters to help. I never heard Grandmother complain of too much work as a child. As her writing attests, she most loved roaming the hills with her beloved little brother, Wesley. The story of the Indians staying and foraging on their land remains true. I wonder if in much later years Grandma ever taught any descendants of that life-saving Native American in one of her one-room schools!

WATER, WATER, EVERYWHERE

Water, Everywhere!
Martin Miller-Hessel

With the exception of 4th grade in New York during my parent's first furlough, I had been educated in a mission school where almost all my classmates and teachers were Filipinos. With their eyes on my eventual return to the U.S. at age 15, Mom and Dad decided I needed some preparatory "Americanization". When I turned 12, they enrolled me in the Boy Scout troop sponsored by the American School in Manila.

I was a raw Tenderfoot when I went on my first camping trip. We went to a park in the mountains north of Manila. The tents went up on a grassy field beside a dammed lake. When we passed inspection, the older scouts paddled canoes to the far side of the lake and I went swimming along the camp-side. Before long   I found myself in a marshy area. The marsh-grass gave me hand-holds, and I pulled my way back to dry land. The mystery of the far side now beckoned. My curiosity outdistanced any good sense I may have had. It didn't look like much of a swim.

Unaware of the invisible flow of water toward the dam, I plunged in. Half way across I began to tire. I realized that I was being pulled toward the dam and the deadly drop beyond. I yelled with fear-enhanced volume and kept up my weakening strokes. What a relief when the canoe-boys heard me and came to the rescue. They delivered me safely back on the camp-side shore… but not without lots of ribbing along the way. I stayed close to our group area for the rest of the afternoon.

After our evening meal, followed by songs, pranks and stories around a campfire, we climbed into our two-person pup tents. Soon an unanticipated tropical thunderstorm opened up on us. Our campsite was transformed into a second lake. We grabbed what we could and raced for the bandstand gazebo where we spent a long night waiting for the rain to stop and the water to recede.

All of us were glad when the sun rose to another clear day. We dried out as best we could and left for home. There we could brag about our great, wet, and brave camping adventure. I never told Mom or Dad about my fool-hardy swimming escapade and fortunate rescue. After all, I was a real Boy Scout now!

PS. *As an adult, I've often wondered, "where were the adult supervisors?" The experience would prompt alert attending when my wife, Pam, and I took family camping vacations and led teen-aged groups on week-long backpacking treks into the High Sierras of northern California.*

Lake Michigan in Winter: 2014
Carole Bos

Far flung sheets of floating ice,
  Captured by bone-chilling wind
Stand at beaches' barren shore
  Now covered with snow and bitter cold.
This Great Lake warped with winter's wealth
  Warns wanderers intent on solitude:
Danger lurks under porous floes
  For fast freezing causes reluctant floors.
No ships, no sound other than cracking ice;
  No color 'cept mottled metal and ivory lace;
No fishermen casting lines from piers;
  Trees stand empty of leaf and shade.
Yet barren vistas yield to beauty,
  As Nature sends such statuary.

How vast we deem the changes of time
  With waves of summer only precious memories.
Then colors danced before our eyes and
  Rhythmic waves broke on sandy shore.
When gull and tern entertained intruders,
  Hoping for cast-off picnic treats.
Raucous sound of child and bather
  Spread across the sandy reaches.

How like life the shore reminds us
  Of feast and famine, brilliance and dross,
Peace and worry, blazing sun and wintry skies,
  Each season lends its wonder to our souls,
A gift breathed in by each beholder,
  Seeking, seeking God's presence and blessing.

"Peaceful" Life on a Dragger (Fishing Boat Culture)
Bruce Calkins

You may have seen the movie or read the book *The Perfect Storm.* It can be both a dangerous and mystical experience to be in a small boat that is dragging a long net over the ocean floor. Our oldest son, David, is something of a fisherman, poet, and philosopher. He started fishing as a summer job while in college and stayed with it (the fishing). David says, "When you're out there in high wind, with the waves crashing over the bow, it's like looking the tiger in the eye." He's out there to see the brilliant sunrises, the thunder storms, the northern lights, and of course, the dolphins, the whales, and the sharks.

That's one side of the fishing culture. Here's another. In the 1980's and 90's, the Provisional Irish Republican Army (IRA) was fighting to force Great Britain to withdraw from Northern Ireland. The IRA was in the market for guns and ammunition. David and his captain were approached by a man in a bar Gloucester, MA. The man offered the captain thousands of dollars if he would take a load of guns and ammunition to another boat that would meet them in international waters. The other boat would then take the arms to the IRA. The captain was excited about earning big bucks in a short time. David had to disappoint the captain by explaining that the man in the bar was an undercover FBI agent, and they'd all wind up in prison. David know the threat of prison would be more persuasive than the ethical argument.

David was out there when a wave crashed through the windshield and shorted out the electrical system. He was out there when his hand froze to the steel railing, and when a cable snapped and knocked out a front tooth. He was 40 miles out one night when 15-foot waves tore the boat apart and sent it under. The crew had time to radio the Coast Guard and climb into their survival suits; however, finding four fishermen in high winds and 15-foot waves in the dark is a challenge. Thank God for the Coast Guard Helicopter Rescue Crew!

Commercial fishing is listed as the most dangerous peace time occupation. Not every risk is from the wind and waves. There is also danger in the very sense of independence and adventure that is part of the fishing culture. David told this story:

"We were sailing out of Portland Maine. We had a crew of 13. There is a rule that no alcohol is allowed on the boat, but we had two cases of beer. We'd been out for a few days when the Coast Guard pulled alongside and came aboard to conduct a safety inspection. They didn't find the beer, but they found that all of our fire extinguishers were flat. They were empty."

I asked, "How did that happen?"

David said, "We'd been using them to wake guys up. When the call went out to get out of bed and get up on deck, some guys just rolled over and tried to go back to sleep. If they didn't get out of bed in time, they'd get a blast under the covers. We'd had enough blasts to empty all our fire extinguishers. Luckily, the Coast Guard didn't give us a citation for having no useable fire extinguishers, and they knew it would be a waste of time to wait for an honest answer to the 'why' question. The bad news is that the very next day, we had a fire! With no other option, we radioed the Coast Guard and told them we had a fire and we needed fire extinguishers. Of course, they sort of knew that already.

"The Coast Guard had to load a supply of fire extinguishers and fly out to the boat. This took time. Fortunately, the fire was confined to the engine room. Finally, the helicopter arrived and lowered the fire extinguishers. We got the fire out, but it had knocked out our engine and our electrical power. After that, we were just drifting and waiting for the Coast Guard to tow us in. There wasn't anything else to do; so we decided it was a good time to drink the beer. Just as we finished all 24 cans, we saw the Coast Guard boat coming; so we dumped the cans overboard. Unfortunately, we were drifting, and the beer cans drifted right along with us. The Coast Guard was not pleased. We didn't catch any fish, so we didn't get paid. This was not one or our better trips."

David and I finished our conversation. We exchanged assurances of love. David said he'd call when he returned from his next trip, perhaps in five days.

I kept thinking about David's story. The Coast Guard crew members were *observers* of the fishing culture, but did they understand it? Did they even want to? How did they describe fishermen to their spouses?

You might find it difficult to relate to a fishing boat culture that uses blasts from a fire extinguisher under the covers as an alarm clock and tries to hide beer cans by throwing them overboard! Nevertheless, I invite you to try this meditation.

The next time you eat fish labeled as "Wild Caught" close your eyes:

-- feel the spray of the wet wind blowing across your cheek,

-- hear the splashing waves and the call of the seagulls,

-- smell the seaweed,

-- and picture the happy fishermen as they gently awaken one another from slumber and sing and dance together as they haul in their nets.

Even the Chaplain Needs a Rest
Norman Stanhope

A Navy chaplain will probably experience his ship going into dry dock at least once in his career. It's a rough time for the ship is torn up, the jack hammers go 24 hours a day, and the men, not always knowing what they're expected to do, become confused. More mental problems arise than any other time.

Our ship was in Bremerton, Washington for a complete overhaul. Bremerton is just across Puget Sound from Seattle. The ship was torn up; the jackhammers went day and night. The noise was so great, I took a little apartment ashore to have some peace and quiet. However, when the ship is torn up the men are torn up too. I always had more mental cases when the ship was in dry dock than at any other time. Consequently, I was tired. The captain let us go early Friday afternoon, so I rented a car (my car was in San Diego) and took off. I went to the ocean, found an Indian resort, and rented a cabin on the water where I could hear the waves hitting the shore. I had a beautiful salmon steak dinner and went to bed. It was great hearing the waves. In the morning, I awoke and walked the shore. Later, I wrote this:

They say man came out of the salt sea--
So it was only natural to return to the sea.
  To cleanse my mind of its frustrations,
    And fears
    And disillusionments.
  For I was tired
    And unconsciously worried
    And afraid.

And so I returned to the sea--
  I heard the roar of the waves,
  I saw rocks protrude from the water like the spine of some prehistoric monster.
  I slept.
  I awoke and walked the beach.

106

The incoming tide tried to draw me back
As though it were drawing me back to the primordium from which I
had come.

And it was tempting.
    Tempting to let the sea cradle me,
    To wash over me and cleanse me.
    Remove all the pains and memories.

For I felt cleansed,
But it was not the time.

For I felt cleansed,
    I felt whole again
Filled with energy to return to what had to be done.
As I left the sea
    I passed through trees
        Tall, shading the road, forming a tunnel,
        A tunnel through which appeared the mountains.
        The mountains which had come from the sea.
        I could see the sea in my rear view mirror.

I thought of the psalmist,
    "I lift mine eyes to the mountain
    From whence does my help come?
    It comes from the Lord."

And I felt new and fresh,
    Cleansed by the sea.
    Challenged by the mountains.
    Strengthened by the Creator.

The Perfect Day at Scotman's Cove
Bill Hansen

Scott Storm is our son. As a son of the Presbyterian Manse we named him Scott, and for a middle name because of a mischievous little neighbor boy whom we came to love and whose family called him Stormy, we named our son Scott Storm. When Scott was 4 months old, diaper and all, I carried him down to the water's edge at Huntington Beach and placed his feet in the briny surf and I whispered in his ear...

"Scott, you are going to love the ocean".

In their later years my parents moved from trailer life in Huntington Beach to the more sophisticated and spacious leisure life of a mobile home and cabana at Aliso Beach in Laguna. The surf break at Laguna, unlike Huntington, is close to shore and the beach drops off in a sharp downward drop so that the waves pounding against the shore create a strong undertow but undertow is different from riptide. Undertow can be very strong but at the same time, unlike riptide, it is short lived because it is counteracted by the swell of the next oncoming breaker.

My parents were very generous with the use of their beach retreat at Laguna and, consequently, Mary Ellen and Scott and I spent parts of every summer vacation enjoying the sun and the surf at Laguna Beach and also on days off throughout the year. Sometimes Scott and I would throw swimming suits and casual clothes into the car and the two of us would head off for Laguna together.

Scott grew up loving the surf. I taught him to body surf at a very young age and when he was ten years old I bought him a surf board. I think that of all of our experiences together on the beach there is one that stands out in my memory as one of the most idyllic days in my life.

We were summer vacationing at our family's mobile home at Aliso Beach in Laguna. Mary Ellen packed a simple picnic lunch and we drove north to the stretch of high cliff that extends between Emerald Bay and Corona Del Mar. Actually at that time it was a deserted stretch of beach owned and operated by the Irvine land Company. At one point along Highway 101 there was a break in the cliffs and a path that plunged down the cliff into a cove that was called Scotsman's Cove. It was a beautiful spot encircled by the cliffs, carpeted with deep white sands and with blue sky whose horizon faded into the intense green of the sea. There was a soft, warm touch to the summer air; a balmy breeze broke the burn of the sun. The sun danced and sparkled on the surface of the sea and there was a surf to kill for. It was just the three of us and as an escape from the calendar and the telephone and the ringing doorbell. It was the most wonderful day filled with a sense of peace and contentment.

Mary Ellen was reading as she rested on a beach blanket spread on the sand. Scott and I eagerly ran to the shore and plunged into the water and dove beneath the white water of an oncoming wave.

The bottom of the shore dropped off dramatically and there was an initial strong pull of undertow. Once we floated beyond the shore break, the undertow lost strength. The waves were shaping up on translucent blue-green mounds of crisp, clear sea. They were large waves, but they shaped up into a sharp clean cut lip that curled over and cascaded in a waterfall of frothy white foam. Scott was floating over the unbroken crest of the waves beside me.

When the waves dissipated I could get my footing solidly on the sea floor below, but the depth was way over Scott's head. However, he could stand on my shoulders and dive into the water and he could hold onto my arms and ride on my back as we dove and splashed and played in the water. I don't remember riding that many waves that day. What I do remember is one of the most idyllic days of my life. I was with the two most important people in my life. We shared a simple lunch on a beautiful isolated beach cove!

Later on I thought of that day frequently, especially after Scott was grown and away at school and I was missing him. Then my thoughts would wander back to that memory of that perfect day.

However, it was many years later when Scott was an adult. We were reminiscing together and I asked Scott if he ever thought about that beautiful day at Scotsman's Cove. Scott said,

"Dad, you know the waves were so huge and we were so far out and way over my head. I couldn't even touch bottom. I was just terrified that day!"

After recovering from my surprise. I laughed and later I thought. Well it's really a lot like life isn't it! Here we are, often surrounded by a sea of overwhelming difficulties that threaten to sweep us away or drive us to the bottom, leaving us gasping for air, weak with striving, and out of our depth way over our heads, and sometimes terrified!

What we fail to recognize is that our Heavenly Father is close beside us, firmly grounded in the bedrock of reality, never too far away to reach out and hold us safe. So now when I think of that day at Scotsman's Cove, the day takes on new and even deeper meaning for me. The memory has become that of a wonderful day that reminds me of the words of the Lord spoken through the prophet Isaiah in chapter 43.

"Fear not for I have redeemed you... When you pass through the waters I will be with you. And when you pass through the rivers they will not overwhelm you...

...For I am the Lord your God.

The Holy One of Israel, your Savior".

It was truly a perfect day at Scotsman's Cove.

The Typhoon of 1945
Ken Grant

The wind shrieked and moaned, flinging salt spray in stinging volleys across the heaving decks of the ship. Fleet tanker A080 rolled and plunged in its effort to stay afloat and keep some kind of control as the typhoon raged. The sky above was a seething canvas of grey clouds, wind tattered and driven from horizon to horizon while below the slate grey sea rose high and fell again into chasms that threatened to swallow the wallowing ship and the fragile creatures who manned her. As one of those creatures, I was clinging to a railing and taking one last look at the fearsome ocean before going below to crew's quarters and such security and comfort as they might afford.

It was 1945 and World War II was still very much in progress. The typhoon had caught the United States Third Fleet and her supply train in mid-Pacific and was playing havoc! The Commander of the train had thought it possible to maintain course, though it meant traveling at right angles to the prevailing wind and seas. This meant that giant walls of water were hitting his ships broadside, causing them to roll dangerously. Looking out to starboard I could see a destroyer rolling and plunging like a wild thing. "I wouldn't want to be aboard her just now, that's for sure!" I said to myself as I grabbed for the handle to the crew's quarters hatch.

Sailors not at duty stations were in their bunks, some reading in spite of the erratic swaying of their quarters. Many had weathered such storms before and were taking it pretty much in stride. But for many, draftees like myself with no previous sea duty, it seemed serious enough. Events were to prove that it was.

The wind increased and the Fleet Commander, seeing disaster overtaking him, finally gave the order, swinging the Train of struggling ships slowly to windward and thus into the oncoming swells. It was a good thing that he did, but it was too late for several of our escorting destroyers. These smaller, lighter ships were more vulnerable to such gargantuan seas. They had rolled too far over, capsized, and gone down, taking their crews with them.

Inside the crew's quarters the thought struck me. "I've got mid-watch on the Flying Bridge tonight!" The thought had been dogging me off and on all day as the seas mounted. The "Flying Bridge" watch meant standing in one of the two gun tubs mounted high on the ship's bridge, wrapped in foul weather gear and keeping watch for heaven knows what! In decent weather it meant a look out for submarines, but in a storm like this it meant misery and nonsense. Who could see anything in this weather anyway... and at night? But, duty was duty, and I was supposed to be there come hell or high water, and it appeared likely to be both.

Eleven Thirty. One half hour to go. I lie in my bunk and feel the ship heel over radically to starboard and slowly back again. Sounds of things rolling across the deck in the officers' cabins located just overhead have me guessing. Suddenly, there is a loud crash on the steel plating just above my bunk! "Whatever that was, it was HEAVY", I thought. The rolling goes on and I close my eyes, trying for just a few more moments of rest before the dreaded watch. Then, five minutes before the hour, I slip into foul weather gear, un-dog the hatch... and step out into the raging night.

Feeling my way along the bulkhead, hand over hand on the railing, I make my way to the ladder leading up to the officers' deck, wishing fervently they had designed this ship with some internal passage from crew's quarters to Bridge. The ladder amounts to what folks back home would call "steel stairs" with hand rails on either side but now wind-swept and glistening wet with salt spray.

I duck my head against the gale and ascend slowly and finally make the top... but no farther... for here the hand rail ends. There is another along the bulkhead ten feet in front of me, but that ten feet is across open deck, cold, grey painted steel as slippery now as glass and tilting sharply from side to side with each roll of the ship, now plunging like a drunken man in a sea gone mad!

Looking to my right I can see, even in the near darkness, the ship's railings. Here, on this deck, they are not a solid rail as below, but leather covered chains hanging somewhat loosely between posts some eight feet apart. If one were to slip on that glistening deck as the ship rolled and head for the rail, the chances of flipping over it and into the sea were high indeed.

Standing there, clutching the rail, my rain gear flapping in the wind and with the rain pelting down, I consider the situation. Is anyone up there in that gun tub now? The ship rolls dangerously over to starboard and even the rim of that high gun tub nearly touches the black and heaving sea before the ship slowly corrects herself and rolls the other way. Praying silently, I slowly turn and inch back down the ladder and along the bulkhead to the hatch. Once again inside I slip out of my gear and climb back into my bunk with mixed feelings. Yet somehow I know that the gun tub on the flying bridge is empty and probably has been for hours, since it's not at all sure that such a place would be safe under such conditions. Braced in my bunk, I doze off.

Hours later, grey dawn has crept across the ocean and the sea has calmed somewhat. Slipping again into my gear I go on deck. The oceans face is still dotted with white caps and the wind is still blowing, though not the gale of the night before. Gazing across the tossing water I spot a "baby carrier" and on her flight deck a mass of tangled wreckage... the remains of aircraft that had been lashed down, only to be beaten to pieces by wind and high water. But it is her bow that catches my eye. It is now covered by a large section of the flight deck that lies collapsed like a wet pancake over the bow of the ship, a testimony to the awesome power of the waves that had pounded her all night. Later, using binoculars, I can see other ships that have suffered in varying degrees as well. Then, needing no binoculars to see it, a grim object appears. We move slowly past the bottom of an overturned ship, a destroyer, capsized and not yet sunken, her keel now barely above water, the waves washing over her. Our crew is silent. Some remove their hats.

Later that day I learn that I had been right about the mid-watch in the gun tub. It seems it had been secured earlier as the storm grew worse. The crew inside on the bridge later reported that, at one point, the ship had heeled over into a 45 degree roll... dangerously far for a ship of that size.

"I was almost walking on the bulkhead", one fellow said.

So the stories grew, as stories will. Years later, swapping sea yarns with other sailors who had been in the great storm, you heard a great many!

One thing is certain: It was a display of nature's power and fury that none of us will likely forget. It is said to have done more damage to Uncle Sam's Third Fleet than any sea battle of the war had done. Sharing stories of the great storm, I was recently told that the great typhoon of 1945 remains the strongest Pacific typhoon ever recorded.

As for the stories that grew out of that stormy night, there is one with which I would like to end this tale... and on a somewhat lighter note. It has to do with that crash I heard above my bunk in the middle of that stormy night while awaiting my turn at watch. That crashing sound I heard was the fall of a homemade still which one of the ship's officers had managed to put together in his room located just above my bunk on the deck above. It was, I understand, a total loss. I doubt that the Captain was ever told!

Bathing in the Artic
Art French

How do you take a bath with no bathroom, no porcelain tub, no running water, no gas water heater? Did you ever think about taking a bath when the temperature is 20 degrees below zero outside! In that case one starts by turning the oil fired kitchen stove up high!

Let's start with water. In the summer we paid young boys 10 cents a bucket (1960's economy) to haul water from the snow-melt-supplied creek across the tundra out back of our home. These 5 gallon buckets of water were then emptied into our 50-gallon oil drum which had a spigot at the bottom. Snow was brought in during the winter. It takes a lot of snow for very little water. There was a very, very large copper kettle-container which we placed on top of the stove in which to heat water for bathing or doing the laundry. Now the water is getting hot. What about a tub?

Some previous missionary had ordered a safari tub. This was a rubberized contraption which could be folded up like a stretcher. Remember? There is no bathroom. So, where do you take a bath? In the kitchen, of course. Place the safari tub in the middle of the kitchen floor, once it is unfolded. From the large copper container on the stove pour in hot water adding enough cold water from the 50 gal. drum to make a comfortable amount of water at the right temperature for a good bath.

Carolyn always preceded me. Ladies first, you know! Then I took my bath using the same water, but we're not done with that water yet. I used it to wash the kitchen floor. What water was left we emptied outside.

Is that all there is to bathing in the arctic? Gracious, no! There is more. I always have preferred a shower. But, remember – no shower; no regular tub; no bathroom. Can't put a shower in the middle of the kitchen. One day while reading the Alaskan magazine to which we subscribed, I noticed a small add for a bush shower head. Great, I thought, here's my chance. This had possibilities. I filled in the order, wrote a check and mailed it off

TO AUSTRALIA!

Finally, it arrived! Hurrah! I could feel that shower already. There were, of course, a few details to which to attend before I actually could take a shower. It started with taking one of our 5 gallon galvanized buckets and punching a hole in the bottom of the bucket. Through this hole I inserted the tube end on the top of the shower head. I added a rubber gasket tightened down with a nut. Before inserting the tube I had placed another rubber washer tightened with a nut on the bottom. Thus, a leakproof seal was obtained top and bottom.

Where to put the shower? There was a fairly good size closet off the study which was near the kitchen and the stove. The toilet bucket was kept in there also. I designed a copper tube circle on which to hang the shower curtain which had been ordered from Sears previously. I hung the copper tube circle from the ceiling of the closet. The shower curtain hung into the galvanized wash tub brought into the closet for the shower. Now about the bucket to hold the hot water: I fixed a large hook in the ceiling centered to the copper tube circle on which the shower curtain hung. To this hook I hung a heavy duty pulley. Then I threaded a long piece of ordinary clothes line through the pulley. I tied the end of the rope to the handle of the bucket containing the water. The bucket was hauled up far enough to clear my head and reach the bush shower head. Strip. Stand in the tub. Adjust the shower curtain. Reach up and twist the shower head. Ah! Feel the water cascading down on me! I'm actually taking my first shower in the arctic! I never used the safari tub again!

Fishing
Ken Grant

The word "fishing" has several possible meanings. It can mean angling for a compliment or some other response from another. It can mean searching for something you just know is buried somewhere in the dresser drawer or it can mean baiting a hook, casting into the stream and hoping to catch a fish. I have done all three, as perhaps you have. What follows is a brief history of and personal reflections upon the latter.

I must admit I do love to fish. Not that I do much of it any more. Life's circumstances have moved me away from the convenient pursuit of that delightful sport. But the memories remain, warm, sunlit memories of bygone days.

I think every child is entranced by fish, whether seen in a fish bowl, a fish pond, or possibly vibrating in the sunlight at the end of a father's fishing line as he prepared to cast his "live bait" out into the mysterious blue ocean or placid lake. There was something almost magical about fish. So it seemed to me when I was young.

It happened at Newport Bay in Southern California. I don't recall the year but I was quite young. Our family friends, the Howells, had taken me along on their summer camping excursion to the Bay. There they annually erected a tent on a rented bay front space not far from the water's edge and there they remained for a month or so, enjoying the sun and sea and getting to know the other regulars of the 19th Street Camp Ground. My stay was not to be long, but it lasted for several wonder-filled days whose memory I cherish still.

The Howells had three boys, one just my age, and we adventured together on what was to become something of an annual event, the trip to Newport and the Bay. However, it was this first trip that introduced me to fish and fishing in a more personal and intimate way. It happened like this…

117

Gordon Howell and I had gone down to the Little Dock (as the 19th Street Landing was affectionately called) to watch one of the local charter fishing boats come in with their load of fishermen and fish. To two little boys from Glendale, it was an exciting moment as the fishing boat approached the dock and made fast. We were fascinated with the warmly dressed men and their burlap gunnysacks heavy with their day's catch, wrestling them off the boat and onto the dock, shouting good naturally to each other as they departed.

Once the fishermen had left, the boat's crew hosed down the deck. Then, opening a cock at the base of the large live bait tank that occupied the center of the rear deck, they allowed its contents to flow out across and over the side and into the bay. Those contents, however, were not only salt water but an abundance of live sardines and anchovies, the live bait, left over from the day's fishing out at sea. The sight of live bait; all those glittering, dancing, vibrating little fish was wonderful! I was entranced! Somehow I managed to grab one before it got into the bay, and I turned and ran back along the bay front toward the tent, holding my live treasure firmly in my hand. I wanted to share it with someone!

As I neared the tent I was aware that my little fish no longer seemed to squirm so strongly. I must have held it too tightly. Arriving at the tent I went to the water's edge and held my little captive under the cool water, but it was too late. Heartbroken, I gave him back to the sea. But I didn't forget the magic of the sight of all those gleaming, dancing fish... and the fact that I had held one, however briefly, in my hand.

In subsequent years, older and wiser in the ways of fish, fishermen and the sea, I baited my hooks and caught mackerel, spot-finn croaker, perch, halibut and even a barracuda or two from the waters of the Bay and others from the Newport Pier. In early days (though long after the above incident) Gordon and I would collect pieces of string and tie them together to make a long enough line to reach the water from the pier's seemingly awesome height. We were more successful in the Bay, however, where access was easier and closer as well.

I recall waking early in the morning, lying in my bed in the Howells' large tent, listening to the sound of the fishing boats heading down the calm, silvery waters of the Bay, their engines making a "chuk! chuk! chuk!" and, disappearing down the silvery Bay leaving a long wake that gradually spread until it lapped gently against the shore in front of our tent with a soft "shissh, shissh, shissh."

Gordon and I would pull on cold, sea-air damp jeans and take the open, wooden kayak, the *Nelly S*, and paddle out over those glassy, silver gray waters and let down our lines, often catching small editions of larger ocean-going fish, especially herring. The Bay was, especially in its upper regions, a breeding ground for many species and thus offered the chance for young fishermen, and often older ones as well, to hook onto halibut or other excellent food fish. There were exceptions, and we always hated the idea of catching a sting ray. Pulling up your line and seeing the gray, frog like head and face of the sting ray rising from the depths was always a bit chilling. We usually pulled them in, cut off their rat-like tail and stinger, and then threw them back to live out their lives without posing a threat to swimmers who might accidentally step on these bottom dwellers of the Bay.

There were years of unusual runs. One year it was baby barracuda in the Bay, mostly no more than a foot or so long, caught in considerable numbers, possibly the result of a rare hatching of this fast-swimming species somewhere up the Bay. Another year it was a run of small mackerel, swarming the waters around the pier over on the ocean side of the Balboa Peninsula on which Newport is located. The Japanese in particular seemed to relish the mackerel and came fishing in great numbers. I was always told they had too many bones, but then, I never ate one to find out. Catching them was the fun! We gave them away.

Ocean fishing, however, gave way in later years to angling for trout, nearly always in Colorado when visiting my many relatives in the Rockies. My sister, seven years my junior, lives there with her husband in Steamboat Springs and has raised three daughters there. Located at one end of the lovely Yampa Valley, Steamboat is a ski town in winter but draws vacationers year round, many to fish the Yampa River which runs through town. My youngest brother, Bruce, is a lifelong and avid fisherman who ties his own flies and wraps his own fly rods. He, who lives in Corta Madera on San Francisco Bay, travels to Colorado every year to fish the Yampa and hopefully, to catch the "Yampa Monster." This is a legendary (in our family) trout living in some deep hole of the river and having escaped countless attempts to catch him, grown bigger and fatter with the years. Presumably a German Brown (they do get big) he probably had a jaw full of old hooks from anglers who have only wide-eyed tales to tell of the "big one that got away." Well, brother Bruce hopes to catch him yet. Who knows? My sister, who expertly cooks the many he does catch, thinks the big one he caught last year was "The Monster" but I don't think Bruce is convinced. Or is the story, and the legend, just too good to give up?

I've fished with Bruce many times leaning on his expertise and having to ask him, rather sheepishly, to help me untangle a snarled reel. But I must confess, it is a very special kind of joy to stand knee deep in the cold, crystal water of the Yampa, surrounded by tall cotton woods and willows, listening to cowbells and the gentle mooing from cows in the pasture nearby. Then, to cast your line over the stream to a quiet hole on the far side and, be it luck or modest skill, have your lure or fly land just where it should; to see a sudden swirl in the water, your line grow taught, the pole bend toward the hole and your reel sing as line plays out. The battle is joined, and your heartbeat quickens. You enter into a special, and I suspect unique, happiness that comes to those who love to fish.

Yes, the settings are a real part of it, as golf links are for those who love that game. In past years I have hiked the mountain trails and through the woods of Colorado en route to streams and lakes that my outdoor loving relatives know and to which they have sometimes led this "city kid" from California. I have slept by a mountain lake close to the embers of a drying fire. I remember a dinner of freshly caught trout, stretched on a green, forked stick and held over the coals, and the can of tomatoes passed around that had first been warmed by that same fire and then eaten with a shared spoon that was passed with the can. I think there were beans, too, but that was long ago.

There is so much more to tell, of floating trips down the river, struggles through dense willows to reach a tiny but trout-rich stream, and on and on, but I share these memories in the hope that you may find some spot, some place in your own memories that resonate with mine.

More fish tales at another time? Perhaps that may be.

ADVENTURES OVERSEAS

Miracle in the Night
Rosemary Pierson

We spent our first year in Brazil in Campinas, a city near Sao Paulo, in Portuguese language study. A fine interdenominational language school was located there. My husband, Paul, and the other men studied in the mornings and I joined the women in the afternoon for classes.

Toward the end of our study, Alice, a recent arrival from the United States, enrolled in the school. A Pentecostal in her fifties, she intended to be a "missionary to the missionaries." She did not seem to be connected to any missionary organization. I am sure she came with a love for God with dreams, perhaps unrealistic, about how she would help. I did not have classes with her and only knew her casually, having greeted her on occasion.

About two years after we had gone to Corumba, she resolved to return to the United States. Wanting to see more of South America, she decided to go by train from Sao Paulo to Corumba, then take the Bolivian train from Corumba to Santa Cruz de la Sierra in central Bolivia, where the railroad ended. From there, she expected to make her way north to the United States. But she had not planned the details of her trip very well.

She boarded the train in Sao Paulo where it left the city of three million and its outlying shanty towns, passing coffee plantations and small towns on the way. As it continued the settlements became more sparse. Small, dry villages appeared. The donkey was a frequent beast of burden. Then mud and waddle houses with small hand tilled gardens, usually including manioc and bananas were seen. In some cases, there were chickens and perhaps a goat. It was subsistence living. The red clay soil left its dust everywhere. Children waved at the passing train.

After two days of travel she arrived at Campo Grande, then on to Aquiduana. There she embarked on the quaint wood burning train that would take her across the "Pantanal," the great Brazilian wetland, to Corumba. Evening was fast approaching.

As the train slowly chugged across the Pantanal on its unsteady roadbed, it seemed to be a precarious journey. (At times there had been accidents in which the train had left the rails). Alice had time to reflect as she sat in the hot muggy air of the train with sparks flying into the open windows. Now she realized that the train would arrive in Corumba, a city she did not know, in the middle of the night. The one thing she did know was that the Paul Pierson family lived there. She began to panic. "What will I do when I arrive?" She thought, "Where can I stay at that hour of the night? Will it be safe? How can I find Paul Pierson?" She correctly suspected that there were no telephones in the town.

She bowed her head and fervently prayed for God to help her find Paul Pierson. Raising her head, she glanced across the aisle and noticed a Brazilian man reading a book. When he closed it she read the title, *Paz com Deus*, (Peace with God) by Billy Graham. Without a pause she jumped up and rushed to the man and asked him in English, "Do you know Paul Pierson?" The man looked up, smiled, and said, "Yes, Paul is meeting me at the train station and I am going to stay at his house tonight." After further conversation Alice returned to her seat, shocked and thankful. She believed she had just witnessed a miracle.

Paul was waiting at the station about 1:30 AM when the train arrived. He saw pastor Eudes coming toward him, accompanied by a woman. Amazed, he saw it was Alice. Eudes, who was the Presbyterian pastor in Aquiduana, had come to Corumba to stay with us that night, then he and Paul were to fly to Cuiaba, the state capital, the next day for the presbytery meeting.

Paul and Eudes took Alice to the Grande Hotel, the only place in town where she could stay, saw her checked in and taken to her room. (She could not stay with us in our two-bedroom house). Previously that week we had met a young American man who had come over from Bolivia and was returning on the morning train. We delivered Alice into his care for the next stage of her journey on to Santa Cruz, Bolivia. Presumably she returned safely to the United States. We never heard from her again.

A miracle? I agree. God gave Alice her own private miracle that night.

Creepy Crawlers and Boiling Water
Rosemary Pierson

Brazil and Portugal provided us with a number of interesting encounters with different creatures. We served as missionaries with the Presbyterian church in those two countries for seventeen years.

In 1956, we moved to Corumba in the state of Mato Grosso in the far west of Brazil. There we found ourselves in the middle of an amazing eco-system, the Pantanal, the world's largest wetland. It was teeming with wild life of all types. The Paraguay River flowed through the area. Dense forests harbored countless species of animals, birds, snakes, spiders, and other insects. Flying, creeping, swimming, biting, running, and jumping creatures were all around us. Hoards of mosquitos and other insects plagued us night and day in the heat and humidity. We could see large tarantulas leaping across the roads at night. I could handle that quite well, but I did not want the critters in our home. Of course, one's wishes and reality are not always the same!!

One hot and muggy Sunday evening the children, three-year-old Steve and one-year-old Kathryn and I went to church for the evening service. We had not lived in Corumba long. Paul was travelling for a few days. Laymen conducted the service. After the enthusiastic service complete with loud singing, I offered to take some of the women and children home. Often people walked long distances to come to church, returning home for them meant walking on unpaved, bumpy roads with no light. Rainy days turned the roads into sloppy mud. We were always amazed at how many adults and children could cram into our jeep station wagon. At times they numbered fifteen or more.

Returning home, Steve ran into our living room to play and I dressed Kathryn for bed. When we went into the living room, Steve had pulled the couch away from the wall and was calling, "Here kitty, here kitty, " and was scrambling around trying to catch something. I saw that it was black and furry, moving quickly and trying to hide. Coming closer, I could see that the "kitty" was really a tarantula, with long, furry black legs. Yelling to Steve to bring me a broom, I quickly put Kathryn in her crib. With great effort I tried to sweep the tarantula out the front door. But it was hopping away and I was hopping after it. I did not want it to hop on me. Our hop dance continued until I was finally able to sweep it out the door, down the steps toward the gate. But it jumped into the yard. I did not want it there near the children. Finally, I settled on a Brazilian technique and sent Steve into the house for two items. Armed with a bottle of alcohol and matches, I got close enough to douse it with rubbing alcohol. I threw several lit matches at it but they were not close enough. Summoning up enough courage to get even closer, I threw a lighted match on it. Poof!! The flame flared up, end of tarantula!

When some of our grandchildren heard this story from their Aunt Kathryn, they gave me a bad time, asking, "Did you really do that?" Adding, "Watch out for Grandma, don't let her have any matches!!"

When we went to Portugal in 1971 we lived in a large house where the seminary had previously held classes. It was surrounded by a very large yard with many weeds.

Shortly after we moved in, a group of young people from the church and their advisors came to spend the day in a retreat. Some immediately went to the kitchen and filled large pots with water and put them on to boil. Then, taking various containers they went into the yard and picked up some objects off the ground, and returned to the kitchen. Soon the kettles were brimming with garden snails. Leaving them to boil for their lunch, the young people returned to their meeting.

I went into the kitchen a bit later and gasped when I saw numerous escapees making their way down the outside of the kettles and on to the counter. I called for help and the snails were soon returned to their 'hot pots.' The report was that they were very tasty. When they were offered to me, I politely declined. The next time the group came the snail harvest was smaller.

Our two younger sons, Sandy and David, played with Andy, a neighbor child, also a son of missionaries. To horrify our boys, Andy would occasionally start a small fire in the yard, catch a snail, roast it over the fire, and pop it into his mouth!

After I had read this story in the class, Bruce Calkins approached me in the Commons, carrying a small white foam plate. Pointing to a dish of cookies nearby, he said, "You don't want those things. Here is a good lunch for you." On the plate crawled a very confused snail.

In 1961, we moved to Recife, Pernambuco, in the poverty stricken north east of Brazil. Paul was a professor in the Presbyterian Seminary of the North, located there. One vacation week we left with Steve, Kathryn, Sandy, and David, driving north from Recife to Fortaleza, Ceara. We went with our friends from language school, Art and Anne Lindsay, and their sons, Arto and Duncan.

We had learned that the Johnson Wax Company owned a home in Fortaleza which was no longer used by their personnel. They had originally harvested wax from a certain type of palm tree in that area but no longer did so. They made the home available to missionaries as a vacation spot. We applied and were given permission to use it for a few days.

Each family drove a Volkswagen bus, or Kombi, over unpaved roads, having to ford small rivers on occasion along the way. As we arrived in Fortaleza we saw beautiful sand dunes on the outskirts of the city. They looked like a wonderful place to climb to the top and slide down.

The house was across the street from the ocean and had a great view. The oblong, U shaped house was wrapped around a three-lane lap pool. We unloaded the cars and Paul and Art went off to see if they could buy some lobsters for dinner. The children went to find garbage can lids and cardboard for sliding on the sand dunes. Anne and I found large kettles, filled them with water, and put them on to boil. Paul and Art returned with several rock lobsters. They are smaller than a Maine lobster but have very tasty meat in their tails.

The men and children went off to slide down the sand dunes, leaving Anne and me to cook the lobsters. Neither of us had handled or cooked lobsters before. We cautiously approached the pots with the wriggling creatures in hand with hopes of getting them into the water. Anne began to shriek and eventually gave up, but finally I got all the lobsters in the pots.

We left the room for a few moments and returned to find the lobsters climbing out of the pots. Obviously they did not like the hot water and we had no lids. Anne did not like it either and to my surprise, began to scream.

When two of the creatures got down to the counter that was too much for her. She ran screaming down the hallway and locked herself in the bathroom, leaving me to get them back into the water. Despite my lack of any proper tools, I eventually got them all back into the pots.

When the men and children returned the lobsters were cooked, Anne had stopped screaming and came out of the bathroom and we were almost ready for dinner. The lobsters were delicious. We laughed and laughed about our lobster tale. The Christmas gifts Anne and I gave to each other that year were dish towels with lobster themes.

Next time, Bruce, just bring me a lobster instead of a snail.

Bering Sea Intrigue
Carolyn French

Cold War time – we've all lived through it - well, not all – because some of the COLD got pretty HOT at times. My husband, Art, and I were vaguely familiar with the HOT international incidents that had occurred between the United States and Russia when borders were crossed. Not long after Art and I arrived as Presbyterian missionaries on St. Lawrence Island, Alaska, we learned that one particular event had remnants (literally) on this very island due to a Navy plane having been shot down and crash landing northwest of the village of Gambell St. Lawrence Island was between Nome, Alaska and Siberia's Kamchatka Peninsula. Being only about 40 miles from the closest Siberian land, the Eskimos on St. Lawrence Island spoke the Siberian dialect. Unfortunately, they were cut off from their relatives and friends due to the Cold War during which no one was to cross the International Date line approximately 15 miles west of this part of Alaska.

In July 1957, when Art and I first arrived, there were six Air Force men in residence connected with the Distant Early Warning (DEW) line. An Army unit was leaving and closing up the base in Gambell. According to a Wikipedia history search report, "At the northeast end of the island there was a United States Air Force Station consisting of an Aircraft Control and Warning (AC&W) radar site, a United States Air Force Security Service listening post, and a White Alice Communications System (WACS) site established about 1952. During World War II, islanders served in the Alaska Territorial Guard (ATG). Following disbandment of the AATG in 1947, and with the construction of Northeast Cape Air Force Station in 1952, many islanders joined the Alaska National Guard to provide for the defense of the island and station."

I served as a public health nurse for the two villages of Gambell and Savoonga on St. Lawrence Island under the jurisdiction of the Alaska Territorial Health Department - before Alaska became the 49th state in 1959! One day I found a brief report that a previous nurse had written about an international incident which had occurred June 22, 1955, just two years prior to our arrival on the island. She reported that, after hearing the distressed plane, the village Eskimos quickly got their boats ready to go to the site of the crash. She planned to go with them, but they talked her into remaining behind and preparing for whatever casualties they would bring into the village.

When the injured arrived she questioned how they had received gunshot wounds. They adamantly denied that they had been shot and gave her other explanations that she had great difficulty believing. One of the military units based in Gambell immediately arranged for a plane to rescue the crew, telling the island nurse that they had arranged transport for all of the crew to a mainland hospital. Therefore, she could stay on duty in Gambell. According to her notes she was very frustrated that for about three days she couldn't find any answers to what had really happened.

Via Wikipedia I located the following information: "On June 22, 1955, during the Cold War a U.S. Navy P2V Neptune with a crew of 11 was attacked by two Soviet Air Forces fighter aircraft along the International Date Line in international waters over the Bering Straits between Siberia's Kamchatka Peninsula and Alaska. The P2V crashed on the island's northwest cape, near the village of Gambell. Villagers rescued the crew, 3 of which were wounded by Soviet fire and 4 of which were injured in the crash. The Soviet Government in response to a U.S. Diplomatic protest was unusually conciliatory, stating that:

- There was an exchange of shots after a Soviet fighter advised the US plane that it was over Soviet territory and should leave (the US denied that the US plane fired at all)
- The incident took place under heavy cloud cover and poor visibility although the alleged violation of Soviet airspace could be the responsibility of US commanders not interested in preventing such violations.
- The Soviet military were under strict orders to 'avoid any action beyond the limits of the Soviet state frontiers.'
- The Soviet Government 'expressed regret in regard to the incident.'
- The Soviet Government, 'taking into account...conditions which do not exclude the possibility of a mistake from one side or the other,' was willing to compensate the US for 50% of damages sustained -- the first such offer ever made by the Soviets for any Cold War shoot-down incident.

The US Government stated that it was satisfied with the Soviet expression of regret and the offer of partial compensation, although it said that the Soviet statement also fell short of what the available information indicated."

Looking back at this bit of history, I am amazed that the Eskimos didn't relate lots of stories about the incident. But I also find it typical of the Eskimos; they do together what needs to be done to meet a crisis and then go on about their daily means of survival. God bless them.

A Jungle Adventure: 1991
K. Roberta Woodberry

Borneo! In my mind's eye it meant "wild men" with blowguns and few clothes, dense rain forests, and danger. But here we were in East Kalimantan (the name now) on a new kind of mission experience.

Our son, John, was a bush pilot with Mission Aviation Fellowship and he regularly flew over the jungle to tiny grass strips carved out of the mountains. He brought in medical and other supplies, personnel, mail, and made emergency evacuations. He also took students out to attend Bible College and to receive other training. But this flight was different. John had arranged with the local pastors in the villages of Long Sule and Pipa Baru to bring Dudley and me on a special visit to see the work there and also to hike to a beautiful waterfall nearby that he could see from the air. They were delighted to be our hosts. They wanted us to spend three days and two nights. He was told that the falls were quite close—only a twenty-minute hike from the main river.

We were all excited as we got ready. Corinne (our daughter-in-law) did most of the planning with help from John, Dudley, and me. Our grandchildren, Katharine and Daniel shared in it all. And before long we were on our way.

From the air, the rain forest looked like it was made of broccoli—yes—broccoli, with some taller trees pushing through to form a higher canopy. Off in the distance you could see villages scattered along the river, tiny swaying footbridges, and the occasional cloud of steam, indicating a waterfall.

As I look back, I can't believe all the "stuff" we took. We must have looked ridiculous to the local folks. We packed foam mattress pads—for sleeping on the bamboo floor of the huts—sheets, towels, filtering water bottles, soap, shampoo, etc. and three large boxes of food items as gifts. We took salt, cooking oil, soap, toothpaste, candy, cookies, sugar, and MSG. (They use that by the handful in their cooking.) Add to that some medical supplies, some children's toys, and some Christian literature the pastors had requested—and we were packed. (You have to be careful about weight in a small plane too.)

We flew in on a beautiful clear morning. It seemed like you could see forever. When we crossed the equator, John jokingly made the plane give a little bump and asked the kids if they could feel it. We all laughed. And then below us was the airstrip. It looked like the top of one of the hills had been cut off and there was this narrow strip ending on one end with a high mountain and on the other end, a thousand foot drop-off led to the valley and the village below. John flew over the field to make sure it was clear of animals and children and then we bumped along that grassy runway to a perfect landing, coming to a stop just before the mountain.

Immediately the plane was surrounded by dozens of children, men, and women of all ages—so excited to welcome us. The children, some in ragged dirty clothes, often hid behind their mothers, but they were curious too. (They weren't used to seeing so many strange folks.) We were introduced to the elderly pastor. He stood about five feet tall and wore a straw, hand-woven hat. But the most unusual sight to me was his ear lobes. The Dayak people put brass rings in their ears to stretch out the holes, and his ear lobes literally touched his shoulder. But his smile was almost angelic. He was radiant. Every time a plane flew into the mountains above their village, Angit, this 72 year old pastor, would hike 1,000 feet up to the runway and pray with the pilot—thanking them for coming and praying for their safety.

He was the one that led the way down the long steep path to the village below. It was wet and slippery. The village men carried our grandchildren on their shoulders and our luggage on their heads. They ran on ahead. But, coming into view before we could get

The swinging bridge

to the village was one of those swinging bridges crossing the rapids of the river down below. The local folks just raced across as if there was nothing to it—but all I could see was the missing slats in the bridge, and the way it was bouncing up and down, and swaying from side to side. Could I do it? After breathing a prayer, and waiting until the motion subsided a bit, I ventured out slowly. One of the elders came to my aid too. He shouted out that there were too many people on the bridge, walking in sync. The bridge was in danger of collapsing. (I heard the translation later, but was delighted that the extra bouncing had stopped.) But where should I look? If I looked down at my feet I saw the water churning down below—but I didn't want to trip or slide into those holes. So I kept my eyes on the goal—the place where the bridge met the land on the other side. As I walked across I could still see the slats, the holes, and hear the rushing stream but slowly, step-by-step I was moving to the other side, tightly grasping the ropes—with my eyes on the goal. (Sounds like a good sermon illustration, eh?)

After I stepped on solid ground I looked up at the village. It felt like I was back in the Philippines. The houses seemed so familiar. They were right beside the river—all up on stilts to protect them from flooding. Most of the homes had stairs chiseled out of logs, but the young pastor's house, where we were to be guests, had real steps and a small front porch.

The stairs to one of the village homes

We took our shoes off at the door and all went barefoot inside. This was a bit hard on my tender feet since the floors were made of bamboo that had been split.. There was some wisdom in that though. You didn't have to use a dustpan and brush. When you swept, everything went down through the cracks.

There were several dogs and lots of chickens living under the floor--providing them a shady place to rest—but it sure was jolting when a rooster (right underneath

135

us) decided it was time to get up at 3:30 am.

Many of the men had gone hunting when we arrived. After the rice is harvested, they go out into the deep jungle. They search for something call "gaharu". I think it's some kind of sap that is used in making incense and is VERY valuable. They also hunt monkeys using their blowguns. The Chinese will pay a fortune for a monkey's gallstone. They believe it is an aphrodisiac. They use the monkeys as a major meat source as well, but I don't know how they preserve them—probably with some of the salt we brought. The dogs love to go hunting with their masters because after a kill they can eat to their hearts content.

Several women were working in the kitchen when we arrived. It looked something like an Old Sturbridge Village, where they reenact early American times. There was a large metal pot bubbling away as it hung over the open fire. It was being stirred almost constantly (I think it was wild boar). There was also a large mortar with a six-foot long pestle where they were pounding something green to pulverize it. My daughter-in-law, Corinne, and I took turns helping.

For supper we sat on wooden benches by a long table and were served a couple of stews—one was chicken and the other wild boar, or maybe monkey—with lots of rice. They even served us boxed cookies, which I'm sure they considered a very special treat.

We all six slept shoulder-to-shoulder on the floor in the living room. We were grateful for our camping mats, but none of us slept too well—the noises of the jungle, the slats in the floor, knowing there were animals right underneath us, and hoping we could make it through the night without having to use the bathroom—all made for a very restless night.

The latrine was attached to the side of the house, down a hallway from where we slept. It was a very simple one. There were two things that made it difficult to use though. The first one was getting there. The hallway we had to go through was where they killed the animals we ate for supper. They pushed the innards and parts they didn't use down through the cracks to the dogs below. But some of the blood and slime was still on the floor and we were walking through it in our bare feet. YUCK!!

The second problem was that the outhouse didn't have a real door. There were some hand-hewn splintery boards nailed together that you sort of held in front of you when you were using the facilities. But they only came up to your neck, (when you were in a seated position) so you could see everything that was going on in the kitchen and they could at least see your head—if they looked your way. You could also see the dogs and chickens down through the cracks—but enough of that. We all survived just fine.

We took our bath the next day in the river—a community bath. I think everyone for miles around came to join us. Corinne and I had purchased in Samarinda the traditional sari-like cloth that you wrap around you for such occasions and the men—at least our men—wore bathing suits. My granddaughter, Katharine, who was five at the time, was very worried that she'd have to go skinny-dipping like the village kids. We reassured her that she could wear her bathing suit, and we all had a blast splashing and washing in the river. Since it rains almost every afternoon, the good Lord provided the shower!

The Waterfall Picnic
K. Roberta Woodberry

This was the day we were all looking forward to—our visit to the waterfall. We all met at the river. I remember there was a light rain, but no one seemed to notice. That was just a fact of life when you lived in a rain forest. The canoes were packed with what seemed to me a lot of baggage, covered with tarps. We were divided into six "katingtings" for our trip up the river. You sat on the floor. In the rear there was a strange motor. It was like an outdoor motor that we knew except for the fact that a shaft held the propeller about five feet from the motor. When we came to rocks or rapids it was pulled up into the canoe so it wasn't damaged. There were four to six folks in each one. We were all seated close to the back, just in front of the driver.

The trees were arching over us like a high cathedral ceiling, providing much appreciated shade in the moist heat. The birds, though mostly hidden were singing their hearts out. Somewhere monkeys were shrieking and babbling as they played together, and of

The katingtings

course, the insects were buzzing loudly too. As I looked around, the beauty of the rain forest began to sink in. Amazing!

The dogs of the village were so excited. They thought they were going on a hunt and they very quickly jumped into the boats and settled at the prow. When their masters told them that they couldn't come this time, they very reluctantly went back to shore—tails between their legs, ears down, and some were literally crying. It tugged at your heart. They too wanted to be a part of it all—hoping of course they'd get some extra meat.

Finally we were off—motors roaring in our long canoe-like boats.

As we slowly made our way up-stream, through several rapids with the jungle holding us in its embrace, I couldn't help but think about what it must have been like for those first missionaries, bringing the Gospel to these remote Dayak people. The river was the only way into the rain forest. They didn't have little planes that could save days of difficult travel. They didn't have outboard motors either. Were they fearful about the Dayak men and their poison arrows? Were they welcomed by these dear people as we had been? Probably not! What did they bring with them? Obviously, they had brought the love of our Lord for now each village had a large simple church and we knew that they felt we were all one in Christ!

After about an hour and a half we reached the trail ending. It had been quite a trip. At one point we had even passed beneath a huge snake coiled around a tree branch. He was enormous—but didn't even twitch his tail when we went by.

We got quite wet wading to shore, but the moisture helped you feel cooler. As I looked at the trail I again thought, "Can I do this?" It went almost straight up a steep incline, and the path was wet, muddy, and very slippery. And then I saw our friends running up the trail, most in bare feet. One man had a generator on his back. What did we need that for I wondered? Katharine and Daniel were lifted onto the shoulders of some young men, and they too were off running. Two other young men came to help me--one on each arm--and two young women came to help Dudley. (He wasn't very happy about that! He wanted to do it himself. He didn't need help from young women!) The old pastor, Angit, was helping Corinne, and they figured John was young and could manage. I kept telling myself that it shouldn't be too bad. After all, it was only a "twenty minute easy hike."

Dudley and I were wearing hiking boots, but Corinne decided that since almost all the local folk were barefoot, she'd just wear her flip-flops. They'd be a lot less trouble in the mud she thought.

I was glad for every bit of help I had! They were so agile and I felt so clumsy. We followed paths along the tops of ridges high up over the river. In some places our guides hacked away heavy vines that were blocking the trail. We fell and slid and slipped. There were a couple of places going down a steep spot where I wanted to just sit down and slide, but my helpers wouldn't let me. I fell at least five times—laughing—and keeping on. We could hear the roar of the waterfall off in the distance, but after twenty minutes we were still slipping and sliding—after forty minutes, the same— after sixty minutes, ditto. I began to think I didn't really want to see the falls anyway—but we were already this far. I COULD DO IT!! After about an hour and a half we finally came to a break in the trees and there it was, about one hundred feet above us cascading into a valley below. It was glorious! I thought of the Garden of Eden. Surrounded by such lush greenery, I wanted to sit and just relax in the glory of God's creation. The faint rainbow, the billowing spray, the roar of the water—our senses were overwhelmed with beauty.

We slid down into the valley at the base of the falls, falling several more times—but my helpers wouldn't let me stop. We had to hurry on. We weren't there yet—and others were patiently waiting for our arrival. We had been very slow. They had chosen a different site of our picnic feast and it was important to them to entertain us there. We had to ford the river twice with the water up to our armpits in some places. Then finally we had arrived. It felt so good to sit on a rock and smell the food being cooked.

* * * * * * * * * * * * * * * * * *

Corinne's feet were not in great shape. Her flip-flops would slide to the side and she had several cuts as a result. At the falls, she went straight to the water to wash the mud away. But what was that black blob on the side of her foot. It wouldn't come off! She suddenly realized it was a leech! She yelled to John for help! He grabbed a machete to cut it off, but Angit, our 72-year-old Pastor, wondered what John was up to—and took the long curved knife away. He simply came over to Corinne and with his fingers removed the leech. His eyes seemed to say, "No big deal! We have these all the time. You Westerners don't know much about the jungle." That was very true!

We did learn something about leeches though. Corinne noticed two more and another stuck on higher up her leg when we were changing clothes back in the village. Dudley beat us all with five. I brushed two off before they could attach, but a third one got me. John thought he'd escaped completely but found a big one when he was changing his jeans. So one lesson we learned about the rain forest, "Watch out for leeches!

140

There are lots of them!"

Back at the picnic spot, things were buzzing. The trek had obviously been a "twenty minute easy hike" for them, for our site was being prepared. A fire was already started and the women who came along were washing and preparing to cook the rice in a big cauldron. The men were whittling poles out of tree branches so that when it started to pour, a tarp was quickly put up using the newly carved poles—and there we sat protected from the torrential rain.

It was amazing to watch it all. Our "paper plates" were to be banana leaves. Two of the women were searing them on both sides in the open fire to kill any bugs (leeches?) and germs. The men were busy catching fish. In a pool beneath the rapids they had extended a net—BUT they used the generator and somehow zapped the fish with a couple of paddles in the water. When they flopped to the top of the pool, they were quickly grabbed while others floated to the net. They threw back the smallest ones, but began quickly cleaning the other fish and started to cook them over another fire in a flat pan. I watched several men carve spoons and a flatter spatula from freshly cut branches. My eyes were popping out of my head. These "primitive" people had thought of everything and with just a few tools had made a tent over our heads and the fire, caught and cleaned the fish, cooked the rice, and were now wrapping the cooked rice in the prepared banana leaves.

Each of us was given a rice bundle. When we opened it on our lap, they came around and put a fish on top. And it was delicious too. They obviously brought some spices along as well. We were served tiny bananas at the end of the meal that were very sweet. I'm still in awe of how they did it! When we were finished, they collected our biodegradable plates and left them in the jungle.

Since they were leaving the spoons they'd made, I asked if I could take one for my spoon collection. I wanted to hang it in my kitchen as a reminder of our awesome picnic adventure and to remember to pray for the Dayak people. They said, "Of course!" but I sensed some reluctance. Maybe they didn't think they were good enough. I thought they were unique and interesting. So, I carefully picked one and carried it back on our "twenty minute easy hike" to the canoe. It was my most prized possession.

But now I had a new problem. Have you ever tried to get into a canoe while standing in waist-deep water? That was my predicament. It was one of those unbelievable situations. How could I get into that boat without tipping it over and dumping all the supplies they were bringing back from our picnic feast? When we had left the village of Long Sule, I had gotten in from a small dock with the help of John and some of the local men, but now? I wished I had a pogo stick and could just bounce up and in. Several of the Dayak men were holding the boat against the rushing current. And several others came to help me. I don't know how it happened—but I made it. They tipped the canoe as much as they could, and somehow I lept up and slid into the back—with help, of course. Fortunately pillows were provided. (The bottom of that boat was not too comfortable—especially when you were soaking wet.) And then we were off.

Getting back was much shorter, especially since we were going downstream. The water and the rapids moved us along quickly and it was wonderful to be able to get out of our katingting at a dock—in a new town, Pipa Baru. While we had been out sightseeing, our luggage had been brought to the new village. When we were taken to our new home, I decided to leave my spoon propped up on the porch until I could get a tissue to wipe it off—and something to wrap it in for packing. But when I returned a few minutes later, my spoon was gone. Did a dog take it for a good lick? Did one of the men take it because it wasn't silver and shiny like the ones they now had in the village? I'll never know. They said they'd make me a new one. But that never happened and I'm left with a memory of a hand-carved Dayak spoon and an amazing picnic. In case you were wondering, I didn't go back to get another one!

The Service
K. Roberta Woodberry

The church seemed huge for such a small village. It was very primitive. It was basically poles supporting a large thatched roof. The rough–hewn benches inside held at least two hundred people. Our family was being honored at this service so we were being ushered down the center aisle; John, Corinne, Katharine (5 years old), Daniel (3 years old), Dudley and me. We tried to sit in the empty front row, but no—we all had to sit on the raised platform at the front, beside the pulpit with the cross behind it. Corinne and I were a bit concerned for the services are very long, and it's very easy to get fidgety—especially for kids. The men were both expected to speak and we all stood to be introduced to the congregation. John and Corinne were both well-known in the village and since they both spoke the language, could help us with what was being said.

John especially had a fun reputation. Not only was he their loved "Peelot Jahn," (Pilot John) flying in their mail, medical supplies, teachers, etc., but they all considered him a "champion." On Independence Day they had had a celebration and for the villagers, the highlight was a blowgun contest. The men all had their hand-made blowguns and they had their own mini-Olympics to determine who would be the champion this year. All the villagers were lined up along the path and then with a strong puff of air, they shot their arrows into the target, several yards away. John was happily watching, when he was told that it was his turn. They couldn't be dissuaded so John stepped up to the line. Everyone started to laugh and cheer, but the village leader shouted out that they needed to be careful. So they quickly quieted down and ALL took a couple of steps back. This novice might not have good aim and they needed to be out of the way. John always had good co-ordination, but he obviously hadn't been practicing those skills on a blowgun. But he was game to give it a try. He took a deep breath and poof, the arrow sped towards the target. There was silence and then a cheer broke out! His arrow had landed on the edge of the bulls-eye. So John was now a celebrity!

When he got up to speak, after Dudley had said a few words, all eyes in the church were focused on him. Corinne and I were struggling though. Katharine and Daniel had started to cry. We were concerned because we were on the podium and knew we were being watched closely too. Finally we understood. We were all covered with biting fleas. There were little black specks jumping all over our legs and clothes. We tried to console the kids and quickly picked them both up and laid them on our laps and out onto the benches—so they weren't in contact with the bamboo floor. We swished the fleas off as best we could. But even as I write about it, I can feel those fleas biting my legs and the old childhood song comes to mind, "The Ants Go Marching One by One"—but these fleas were coming at least "ten by ten," and with a vengeance. We had brought along some insect repellant, but that didn't help since it was back in our suitcases. The folks in the congregation didn't seem to be having a problem either. I don't know if just the platform was infested, but it was awful. I tried hard to smile when someone looked my way, but I'm afraid I just wanted to get away from all the stinging, itching, and biting. And basically that's what I remember about the service.

At the end we were presented with gifts—hand-made baskets (actually basket-backpacks) that had been woven out of special reeds. Mine has Roberta woven into the design. Dudley's has his name too.

I feel so badly as I look back on that experience. So often I let something interfere with my worshipping the Lord, even when I try not to…and I had been so looking forward to sharing with these dear Dayak Christians.

Pastor Angit gave Dudley and John each a beautiful machete that he had made at his own forge and then carved the elaborate bone sheath. It was fascinating to watch him work in such a primitive way. That's how he earned his living. He was a Pastor on the side.

There were lots of folks that followed us up the mountain trail to the airstrip for our trip back to Samarinda, where John and Corinne had their home. Pastor Angit prayed with us, as was his custom, before we left, and then we were roaring and bouncing down that grass strip. It was an unusual takeoff, and John had warned us about it. The runway wasn't really long enough, so when the runway ended, the plane dropped down toward the valley floor before it began its slow climb up above the rain forest. We "bounced" over the equator on the way back and laughed again. And then we were back landing on a real runway and being welcomed by the maintenance crew and the hangar dog—a lovely lively rescued mutt.

I can't close though without telling of another experience we had before we returned to the States. We all loved Indonesian food. It is quite similar to Thai and we stopped at a large noisy restaurant, known for its delicious satay. Our family was seated on a small platform—like a raised floor—with pillows and a small table in front. Our meal was wonderful. Then Daniel said something like, Watch!" We all turned to see him shoot one of the wooden satay skewers across the restaurant—over the heads of the other patrons. He'd cleverly made his own blowgun by putting the skewer inside a drinking straw and poof—off it went. It was so hard not to laugh and fortunately, he hadn't hit any of the other diners. He later got to practice his blowgun skills in a safe place—his own backyard.

P.S. Mission Aviation Fellowship is still flying into those villages bringing needed supplies and sharing together in their love of our Savior.

And "That's all for now!"

SHIFTING GEARS

We Are All Immigrants
Gloria Shamblin

I had travelled from London, stopping at New York and San Francisco, finally arriving hot and tired at Los Angeles airport. On the late August day, it felt hot and dry and the airport had an alien smell completely different from the country I had left. I was immediately homesick, but had promised myself I would stay for a year and then I might be ready to go back to teach in tough inner city English high schools. To work in the United States, I had visited the American Embassy in London, filled out forms, had a physical and a chest x-ray and now I was eligible for a green card.

A year passed and then another and then several more. I found jobs, met friends, got married and had two sons and many more years passed. The subject of U.S citizenship came up occasionally. I was wary of confiding in anyone that I was not a citizen. It seemed being an immigrant was often associated with second class citizenship. There was a lot of confusion in the general public regarding legal and illegal citizenship. I paid taxes, worked, obeyed the law and had a green card, which now incidentally had been changed to a pink coloured card. Of course I could not vote and was fairly ignorant of how the United States government system worked. I learned some American history when my children came home from grade school. As the woman in the street I could name the President and for how long he would be in office. The rest of my knowledge was sketchy.

I had a lot of struggles within myself trying to decide on citizenship, as I still loved the country of my birth. I could not talk with my English family, as all my uncles had fought for my freedom in the Second World War and my father had been killed in the fighting. I would be considered as "selling out". I reviewed every passport I had kept since I was 16; did I want to give up this citizenship? I am not quite sure what the turning point was but at the time of my decision I was taking tax preparation classes. A class member told me it might be easier for my family in the United States to settle my affairs if I was a U.S. citizen and I became incapacitated or died.

I had made my decision, and since I like doing detective work, I decided to do some research to see how well I could answer the questions to qualify to be a British citizen. I passed, but not with flying colours. A couple of the multiple choice questions were interesting. What is the dried fruit and spice pudding served at Christmas? Is it Yorkshire pudding, Dumplings or Christmas pudding? That was easy. What is the location of Santa Claus, The South Pole, and North Pole? Poland or Ireland? There were questions on dialects, these were tricky. Where do they speak scouse? I knew this was Liverpool.

I cannot remember how I set about my United States citizen quest but I do know it was long and involved. I had to find many documents, recall many dates and fill out many forms. These included birth certificates, marriage and divorce papers, even something called a Deed poll where I had changed my last name as a combination of my father's and stepfather's surname

Of course there was "A Guide to Naturalization", and a study guide, lots of government information and test questions. My son and I laughed over it. Who was here before the Americans? was it Canadians? Native Americans? Or no one? Did the pilgrims come over on the Mayflower, the Santa Maria or the Titanic? Did I want to become a citizen so I could get a credit card, a driver's license, or to vote? There were sample civics questions for elderly applicants and for residents who had lived here for 20 years and were over 65; requirements were different and they could also be tested in the language of their choice.

There were numerous interviews and several fingerprint sessions. The appointments were all at out-of-the-way locations and at very early morning hours, with no available parking ever close at hand. When I reached the venues there were long lines. I was born British, so I knew how to queue, not everyone else did. Usually the people that got to the front of the lines were the attorneys who had previously completed paperwork at a price for numerous clients. Many of the people did not speak English and I felt very sorry for the older people that would often appear bewildered. They did not seem to know exactly why their families had brought them there. I had not read all the fine print on all the documents that explained many people were considered exempt from speaking English and they could still become citizens. Finally, the day came for my interview. I was very nervous and some of the questions were difficult. I could not repeat the answers today.

My interviewer had lots of questions for me about England.

Eventually the day came for the swearing in. I was allowed to take one friend with me and I chose my good friend Margaret McAustin. Not only was she a wonderful friend but very civic minded and to me the very best representative of United States citizenship. So along with 9,000 other people that morning of May 22, 2002, I was sworn in at the Pomona fairgrounds as an American citizen. I was given my Naturalization certificate, a small flag, and a book welcoming me to U.S.A. citizenship. So now I could vote and serve on a jury. I do the former. I have been called for jury duty; one of the many called but never chosen. Being a citizen gave me the courage to take classes and become a Notary Public.

I have kept all the citizenship documents, all my passports and my original green card so that my grandchildren can trace back their roots. Since I was a child I had always thought it would be good to be a world citizen, but as far as I know there is not a passport for that. Today I can listen to the National Anthem for both countries and have a tear in my eye for either... I am fortunate to have had citizenship of two great countries.

A Lucky Family Scheme
Norman E. Thomas

1949 proved to be the most important year of my adolescence—a year of change and challenge for me. Fortunately, I felt, I had decided upon graduation to attend Drew University in Madison, New Jersey, outside New York City. Drew offered scholarships to children of Methodist clergy in the New Jersey Conference. I applied in my sophomore year and got early acceptance with full tuition scholarship for my four years of planned studies. I had not thought of going anywhere else.

The process of applying to colleges in the 1940s was very different from the challenges faced by my grandchildren in recent years. We tended to apply to only one college at a time. In my junior year in high school my older sister Joan applied to Duke University but was not accepted there. Her second choice was Drew. And it would be an easy driving distance for her boyfriend Walt Jacoby from Lafayette College where he would be. Joan agreed to apply to Drew **if** our father would persuade me to go to some other college. Our parents expected us to get good grades and I, in high school, got the best grades in the family. Joan didn't want that family comparison to continue through college.

My high school graduation photo

"Norman," Dad said to me as I started back to high school for my senior year, "do you realize that you've never looked at different colleges, but only at Drew? I'll take you to visit some others." "Okay.," I dutifully replied. In the next weeks we visited Haverford, Lehigh, and Ursinus colleges in eastern Pennsylvania. I recognized that they were good schools, but replied that I still wanted to go to Drew.

Behind closed doors, I learned later, my parents felt stymied. They had pledged to Joan that I would not attend Drew. That week Dad shared his dilemma with Fred Fox, a leading lay person in the Haddonfield church.

"Why don't you take Norman to visit my alma mater—Yale University?" Fred replied. So in early November Dad and I went up to New Haven, Connecticut.

Yale seemed different. On the prospective student tour we learned about the college system at Yale. About 300 students lived together in each residential college beginning in the sophomore year. Each college had its own dining room, library, commons, and affiliated faculty. Yale offered both the advantages of a large university and the opportunity for deeper personal friendships. The student tour leader, who was himself on scholarship, shared that Yale offered generous scholarships and opportunities to do meaningful work to cover almost all the costs of room and board. Furthermore, almost all students entering Yale College graduated there. I returned home eager to apply to Yale, to the relief of my parents, and Joan.

In those days Yale sent separate letters to applicants from the admissions and financial aid offices. Mine arrived on consecutive days the next April. First, I opened the admissions office letter and jumped for joy. I had been accepted. That joy lasted just one day, for the next day I received the letter from the financial aid office with the words, "we regret that we are unable to grant your request for financial aid." In tears I recognized that I could not attend Yale without such help. Fortunately, I had been accepted with scholarship by Drew University, now my second choice. I would go there.

Not until forty years later did I learn what consternation took place behind closed doors that night as Mother, Dad, and Joan digested this outcome. The next day Dad shared the sad news with Fred Fox, our Yale friend. Fred responded: "Ernie, I have an idea. I'm a member of the Philadelphia Yale Club. It also offers scholarships and I know the chair of its Scholarship Committee. I will appeal to him for help." Fred did so and reported back to my dad: The chairman said that the Scholarship Committee has already met and made its awards for the fall semester. However, they do keep some funds in reserve. Although they will not meet again before fall, if Norman would go for an interview to the office of each committee member, they could consider his late scholarship application.

I had a most unusual graduation day from high school. That morning Dad drove me to downtown Philadelphia. He waited patiently as I took elevators up tall buildings to be interviewed in the offices of bankers, lawyers, and corporate executives—the members of the Philadelphia Yale Club's Scholarship Committee. The next week they announced their decision. Yes, they would grant me a one semester pre-ministerial scholarship. If I chose another career, it would become a loan. When they reported this late scholarship to Yale College's Financial Aid Office, they learned that Yale would give me, as a scholarship student, both work-study and rent reduction to cover most room and board costs.

This chapter of my life had a very happy ending. Once at Yale College I received full scholarships and creative work-study opportunities all four years. I continued on my vocational path to prepare for ordained ministry. And my sister Joan completed her studies at Drew University and married Walt. What had taken place in our house behind closed doors without my knowledge turned out to have been for me a lucky family scheme.

The Rise and Fall of Interests
Robert Bos

Have you ever asked yourself the question, "Why am I still doing this?" It may be something that you had been doing for quite a long time and suddenly you asked yourself that question. It could have been an interest that was very useful to you at one time, anything that you needed or wanted to do, but for some reason it became no longer important to you. So why do it any longer?

Bruce Calkins, a fellow writer in our writing class, asked himself that question in a story he told to our class one day. Bruce is an avid mountain climber. He was beginning to think that maybe he was getting a little too old to continue doing what he enjoyed so much. Although hiking was strenuous exercise, it was a good question to ask himself. He recalled how he occasionally would exchange brief greetings with other hikers on the trail. Something more meaningful did happen to him one time. He engaged in a longer conversation with one hiker whereby the new friend learned that he was a minister. That lead to the man sharing some of his problems and the whole experience ending with a prayer. It made Bruce have something to think about when asking himself the question, "Why am I still doing this?"

When he shared this with our class, he triggered a question in my mind. There were several times, one leading into another, where I had been asking such a question. Over the years they came in this order; learning to play the piano, learning to speak German, writing two children's books, and then back to learning to play the piano. One can see that for me, at least, it is an often asked question. I began taking piano lessons at an early age but it didn't last very long. I picked it up again in my adulthood but life just became too busy for me to continue. I found myself asking, "Why am I doing this?"

The rise and fall of interests. My intent to learn the German language was my next big challenge. I had taken a year or two of German in college but seemingly that was just part of my liberal education. My greatest incentive came when our son Stephen attended the DLI, the Defense

154

Language Institute in Monterey, CA as part of his preparation to serve in Army Military Intelligence. This presented a challenge for me to become a better student of the language so that we could converse together. While he was away in Iraq and Germany, I took weekly lessons from a neighbor friend who retired as a high school instructor in German and Spanish. Also, at this time I was active with the Berlin Fellowship, which was an informal relationship between the Evangelical church in Germany (East) and the Synod of Southern California and Hawaii. It had to do with the experience of American and German Christians in post-war Europe and Berlin and parts of the East. In the summer of 1983, I was part of a team to assist in the recovery as a sign of reconciliation. My ability to speak German was helpful.

After we moved from Westlake Village to Pasadena, I attended weekly classes in German taught in a German speaking church in Glendale. Further, while on staff at Bel Air Presbyterian Church in Los Angeles, I began a partnership between the Bel Air congregation and a church in former East Germany. This proved to be a rich experience as people from both congregations visited each other in Germany and the USA, shared faith, and became acquainted with each others' culture.

After I retired, our son had returned home and became very sick with cancer and died at age thirty-four. After my rich experience with the German language, I began to lose interest in experiencing further use of it. I had no further need for it. Being retired in Monte Vista Grove Homes there were few people who had any familiarity with the language. I began to ask myself, "Why am I still doing this?" I occasionally hunger to delve into it deeper but I ask, "Why?" I have lost my incentive, my motivation to further engage in it. With Steve gone and my earlier German relationships nonexistent, I felt the need to move on.

My next thinking led me back to the piano. I wanted to pursue a fresh attempt at this. It was still one of the things that I wanted to do with my life, to learn to play the piano. So I bought a keyboard with intent to try again. That started well but then a new interest challenged me more. That inspiration came out of the writing class I attend. After writing a paper for the class entitled, "Walking the Trail," the instructor suggested that I might want to consider making it into a children's book. With some revision and encouragement, it evolved into a story about Billy and his gift of imagination. After this book was published, I was motivated to write another, this being a companion story on the gift of curiosity. That, too, has now been published. With that accomplished, I presently have no new interest so I am returning once again to my unfinished task of learning to play the piano, via the keyboard. Will some new interest again capture my attention? Who is to know? Why am I still doing this? The question makes life exciting and interesting. So it is with the rise and fall of interests. It is all a part of life's transitions.

A New Career
Mary Froede

After working for seven years at Arcadia Methodist Hospital I finally saw "the writing on the wall" and on my paycheck, and realized I had no opportunities for advancement there. Also, a breeze of adventure had tickled me and I decided I wanted to work in downtown L.A. Off to the want ads. The most intriguing was the one which offered a position as a legal assistant in a U.S. Custom's law office in the World Trade Center, a fairly new high rise in downtown. I applied, and amazingly got the job. That experience is a whole different story than the one I want to tell.

While I worked there, we watched the five towers of the Bonaventure Hotel rise on the horizon. I developed a friendship with a lady who also was an adventurer. She had garnered $10,000.00 to build a kiosk in the lobby of the Trade Center where she would sell items made exclusively in California. The Trade Center housed many embassies from small countries, and their employees traveled a good deal on business. Often they only flew "red eyes" for overnight meetings, and carried an overnight case with maybe just a change of shirt and socks. The items that Beverly included in her shop were often too big or too expensive. One day at lunch she informed me that unless she had some small, touristy items to sell, she was going to have to shut down. As I have always loved crafts, I offered to come up with some items that might sell. For a year, while still working full time, I sat at my sewing machine or silk-screened on my dining room table every weekend. My husband, Jim, used to tease me and say that if I behaved he would undo my handcuff from the sewing machine and let me out for a little while. The results were head scarves, logo tee shirts, short skirts, and full-length pool dresses. I also made aprons and placemats.

After getting production pretty well started, Jim and I took our usual month's vacation to Europe. When I returned, buried in the pile of mail was an order from a lady in Palm Springs who owned and operated nine golf pro shops in the desert. She ordered a full line of the clothing for each of her shops. I gave my notice at the law office and shackled myself to the sewing machine. With this initial order, plus $100 of grocery money, Klever Kuvers was born.

I nosed around a lot at that point to find out how to market my products. My mother always had worn an apron and had many that were patterns from my grandmother's era. I modified them to "modern" use and created them in lovely floral and printed calicos. The best way to market them was by exhibiting in various food shows. I did so, and soon had a line of items for sale all over the nation. My apron line was featured at leading department stores (Bullock's, Broadway, Robinson's, and Mervin's) and many "mom and pop" stores. I exhibited in Chicago, Dallas, San Francisco, and Los Angeles.

At one of the shows, a man approached indicating that he was from Monarch Foods. He asked if I could manufacture a particular butcher's apron in vinyl. I said I was sure that I could and proceeded to make some samples in vinyl for him. He liked them and became a customer. A number of months later, he called and indicated that he had taken a new job. I was alarmed as he was a big customer for me. He then told me that his new job was as a buyer for "Taco Bell". The rest, as they so blithely remark, "is history". Next, someone from the managing company of Taco Bell called to say that they wanted vinyl **tablecloths** for their 286 "Chevys" restaurants nationwide. We manufactured those for many years, but they finally bit the dust and had to declare bankruptcy a few years ago. Recovering from that was difficult, to say the least.

I have never advertised or had a company web site. I don't even list my telephone number… but word of mouth is a powerful thing. I now supply wholesale vinyl aprons to seven warehouses from California to Florida. These warehouses list my aprons in their catalogs, allowing individual restaurants to purchase them. One of the managers from Chevys who had left and taken a job at Red Robin, called and decided he wanted to put red vinyl tablecloths on their patios. Because of weather conditions, only the west coast so far has signed on. Again, from word of mouth, I have almost 50 customer restaurants in California, Oregon, Nevada, Arizona, and Colorado. As of this writing, my sales have spread as far east as Missouri.

It has been a wild 40-year ride and I am still at the helm. I will be 87 years-old next week. After approaching a broker and exploring the possibility of selling the whole shebang, I finally tried to convince my daughter to learn the business and take over when I can no longer provide the good service that I have always given. She absolutely refuses as she has her own business that she loves. I have contacted a business realtor. We'll just sit back and wait to see what happens.

ALL IN THE FAMILY

The Dishwasher and the Workbench
Robert Bos

My wife and I appreciate orderliness. That is the gold standard of being good Presbyterians: to do things decently and in order. It is important to us that each day the beds are made, the house is mostly clean and picked up, and everything is in working order. Basically, we are ready to receive unexpected guests at most any time. We probably inherited this trait from our Dutch ancestors who scrubbed the streets with brooms and water. This practice is enacted in my home town of Holland, MI each year in the Tulip Time parade when the main street is scrubbed clean.

In spite of this obsession for tidiness in our home, there are two household commodities upon which we have differing views as to how to handle them. They are the dishwasher and the workbench. I am perhaps a little phobic when it comes to filling the dishwasher. It is important for me that each item loaded into the machine has its proper place and position. This is necessary to allow for the best use of space and efficiency. It only makes sense that cups and saucers, bowls and pots, spoons, forks, and knives, and other utensils be put in their proper place. Such fastidiousness comes to the awareness of my wife when I occasionally try to improve on what she has done. There may be a cereal dish that needs to be turned over so that it doesn't fill with water. Haste can allow these things to happen. For the sake of this writing, I asked her how she felt about this. She surprised me when she said that she didn't really care. Every wife that she knows asserts that their husbands do the same.

The other household fixture upon which we have differing views is a workbench. This situation became evident in the home we lived in before we moved to our present, smaller location. The workbench was located in our garage. It was made by my wife's father on one of his visits to CA. My wife remembers his workbench at the home where she was raised in MI. It, too, was in the garage but it was large, with all kinds of electric saws and highly organized drawers with a great variety of assorted screws, nuts and bolts, washers, etc. It was beautifully organized and equipped. One can imagine my wife's standards for our little workbench. On one end of it was a small vice. Above the bench was a pegboard with moveable hooks upon which could be hung smaller items. Also, on the bench there was a small tower consisting of drawers in which an assortment of nails, screws, washers and other small items were easily obtainable. Everything was nicely organized until, in time, it became a mess. Little was put back where it should have been, tools and parts were difficult to locate. Screws were no longer sized in their own drawers, bits for the drill were scattered about, and nuts and bolts were intermixed with washers. It became a point of frustration for my wife. I began to hear her say, "I wish that you would do something about that workbench. I can't find anything." As I recall, I may have made some feeble attempt to put things back in order, but my heart really wasn't in it. To me, it was not that important. It did take a little longer to find things but it was still a workable situation. It was not good enough for my dear wife so she took it upon herself to reorganize it once again.

It was a recurring situation even after we moved to our smaller quarters in Pasadena. We had to downsize in everything, including our tools. Everything had to be put in a medium size toolbox. Some of the bigger items were placed in a cardboard box of about the same size. A nice feature of the toolbox is that it has a tray with a handle so that it can be removed and carried to a location where a small repair needs to be made. There is room for such items as a small wrench, pliers, screwdriver, etc. Unfortunately, even in this smaller space with less equipment, clutter has returned. It is difficult to find things. We both agree but will I do anything about it?

So it is that my wife and I are so well ordered when it comes to the general state of our house and yet have differing views on managing and maintaining our two household commodities: the dishwasher and the toolbox. If I were asked how I feel about this, I would probably say, "Not enough to do anything about the toolbox. On the other hand, maybe I will surprise her and put it in order and try to keep it that way. She's still waiting.

A Baby Bump
Mary Froede

I read the "pulp" magazines at the doctor's office and the beauty shop, including *People, Us* and other magazines of the same ilk. I am always amazed at how many pictures are presented of the various movie/TV actresses showing off their "baby bump". These particular women take delight in showing their protuberance sans clothing and have those self-satisfied looks on their faces. How many of you ladies can remember how diligently we draped and swathed our bodies until the baby was born in order not to expose our "baby bump" to prying eyes? Why couldn't we have just worn a burkha? We could nowadays as we are certainly seeing more of those in our daily lives. Actually, one of the valid reasons for "concealment" was the fact that you were relieved of your job at the first mention of pregnancy. Also, any discussion of that subject was usually in a whisper. I held on for about four months, but I worked for a doctor and he was well aware of my change in personality at that point!

I first became aware of the fact that I was pregnant at age 22, and had been married for most of a year. I was seriously cautioned by my mother and many friends to not tell anyone until I started to *show*. They said the nine months seemed like eternity when everyone knew early on. Imagine how dreadful that must be for an elephant. As skinny and small as I was, it was easily my sixth month before I could no longer struggle into my regular clothes. Besides, I was so excited and proud of my current condition, that I *wanted* to share my joyous news with others. I slipped into my flowing tent-like maternity gowns with ease and rather enjoyed their fullness on the hotter days. One day though, my husband, Jim, came home to find me in the bathtub, *au natural*, with the TV pulled into the doorway. Now that was really cool!! The slacks we wore looked like the pants a clown would wear in Barnum and Bailey's circus except for the obvious front panel almost absent.

Now, it seems that women wear T shirts that ride up *above* the "bump" and slacks that slide *below* said "bump" with nothing to interfere with the resulting view. They remind me of the comic male figures that wear their belt *below* the protuberance in order to boast a 28" waistline. I, on the other hand, struggled to cover it all up as was the custom at the time.

Now, dealing with my current "bump", which is obviously not due to pregnancy, is the delight of sitting down and having that convenient shelf on which to rest my magazines, books, dinner plates etc. You all know the drill.

What brings all of this to mind is the fact that having developed a "bump" in my old age cannot be considered anything but being overweight. My husband once said that I had an hourglass figure, but that the sand was going to the wrong end! I make every effort to hide it by wearing clothing that could have passed for maternity wear when I was young. Struggling in our workout room periodically, I use the machine that is supposed to reduce the belly and strengthen the back to be able to counterbalance what is up front. I don't seem to be having much luck in that department, so I console myself with the knowledge that my mother, father and, husband had dwindled down to almost skeletons by the time they left "the mortal coil". So... my new philosophy of life is that I have something comparable to the camel's hump. When I start deteriorating, I will have this "bump" to fall back on and use at its own discretion.

My Special Outfit
Laura Berthold Monteros

When I was in junior high and high school, The Beach Boys shone at the top of the charts like the noon sun over the blue Pacific. With songs like "Surfin' Safari," "Surfer Girl," and "Surfin' USA" running through my mind and my inner self-image of having surfer-girl straight hair and riding the waves, you might think that I surfed all the time. I didn't. I stayed with a friend at her beach house once and she had promised to teach me, but the water was too choppy so her dad limited us to body boards. That was the end of my surfing career.

The surfer culture mingled with the Valley culture, and a drive through the McClure Tunnel to Santa Monica or over the hills to Malibu and Zuma was an oft-made trip for those with cars. There was a well-known surfboard shop within a couple blocks of my high school. Boys sported bleach-blond hair, and everyone wore flip-flops (though we called them thongs or zoris). But for me, the most sought-after item was a surfer shirt.

A surfer shirt was a regular T-shirt with broad stripes in white and a single color—blue, red, navy, yellow, or green. I wanted one. Oh, how I wanted one, in green, my favorite color! But they were more expensive than regular T-shirts, and most girls didn't wear T-shirts too often in those days. We had to wear dresses or skirts and blouses to school, church, and most other places. My mother made most of my clothes except jeans and jackets, and splurging was not allowed.

I went all the way through high school without ever knowing the joy of wearing a surfer shirt. I graduated in June of 1965 and cast around as to what to do now that I had to make my own decisions. I had a lot of acquaintances from my classes and the youth band I played in, but I always felt like the odd one out.

One August evening—it happened to be my 18th birthday—a friend from youth band and I were going out. I was probably the driver, having both a license and an old Opel. My friend had to get something from the drum major, so we stopped by his house on the way. It turned out that was the real destination.

"SURPRISE!" about 25 people yelled as I walked through the door. My bandmates were there, along with a few friends from school, including a boy I had a crush on. I got tossed in the swimming pool. We had food and cake and pop, talked and danced and got to know each other after knowing each other for years.

There were even gifts! The boy I liked gave me two LPs, which would have been a pricey gift if they hadn't been freebies that his musician father had gotten. A girl who had won the position of high school drum major, only to have it snatched away because the Girls Vice Principal refused to have a girl singled out on the football field, gave me jewelry.

There were a few other things, but the best gift, the very best gift ever, was a green-striped surfer shirt that several of my friends had chipped in to buy. I could hardly believe this coveted item was finally mine. And I was surprised they knew how much I wanted one. I must have talked about it more than I realized. And more surprisingly, they had listened.

By the time my 19th birthday rolled around, my life had changed drastically. My friends and I pretty much lost contact, but I still had the shirt and continued to wear it for years. I stopped when I realized that it wouldn't take too many more washings before it deteriorated, but I kept it. I kept it because it reminds me of so much more than The Beach Boys and dreams of surfing and a wish fulfilled.

It reminds me of a night when I drove up unsuspecting to a house at dusk and had the time of my life with people who liked me enough to throw me a surprise party, despite all my social inadequacies. It reminds me of the close friends who cared enough to know the one thing I really, really wanted and to get it for me. It is a tangible remnant from my last hurrah between high school and adulthood. Though my life was never simple, this garment is a symbol of how much simpler it had been than it became, and it occasionally causes me to muse what my life would have been like if I had made different decisions.

I don't spend more than passing seconds in contemplation, however. Such thoughts are bittersweet, but they are not too productive this many years down the road. The life I have now is *my* life, not the life I imagined when I was 13 or 15 or 17, but one made from a mixture of my choices, the choices of others, and circumstances beyond choice. Still, when I go through a box or a drawer to cull out clothes and find this shirt at the bottom, I stop for a bit. And I put it back.

I still have that surfer shirt.

Tennashoes
Laura Berthold Monteros

When I was a kid, there were three kinds of shoes: dress shoes, school shoes, and tennashoes, pronounced to the spelling T-E-N-N-A-S-H-O-E-S. There were only three kinds of tennashoes: red Keds, blue Keds, and black hightops. Girls wore red Keds and boys wore blue Keds or hightops. I once teased a neighbor boy because his mother had bought red Keds, something I felt very bad about later and wished I could have taken back.

At some point, white hightops became available, or maybe they always were, but my family only bought black. My brother, who is five years older than I, wore hightops, and I loved them with a passion only Imelda Marcos could understand. I loved the way the canvas curved up to the ankle, I loved the extra grommets and longer laces, I loved the round rubber circle at the ankle bone that we all knew gave extra protection, I loved the thicker soles which could undoubtedly make me jump higher. My dream came true when my aunt took me shoe shopping, and over the objections of the shoe salesman, bought me the prized footwear. (*Nota bene:* A shoe salesman was a person, usually a man, who measured your foot, suggested a size larger than what was measured to allow for growth, and retreated into the arcane alcove behind the shoe display to return with boxes of shoes in the correct size and style. I think they are extinct.)

It was my turn to be teased on occasion, but since I could beat up every boy in the neighborhood except Tommy Slauson, I ignored it.

As I matured, I learned that tennashoes were really *tennis shoes*, worn when playing tennis. I was told by a shoe maven that what kids wore were not really tennis shoes and should be called something else. I'm not sure what, though I was aware that some people used the word *sneakers*, mostly adults and boys who imagined they were wild Indians or detectives and could sneak up silently on unsuspecting people, usually girls. It seems to be the word of choice now.

In junior high there was a fashion explosion for sneakers in all colors of the rainbow, and it suddenly became fashionable to wear them as school shoes. Some girls stocked up; I believe I only had two or three colors. I liked the élan of multi-colored sneakers, because up to that time I had worn brown oxfords in an attempt to correct pigeon toes. (*Note bene:* Pigeon toes aren't corrected by oxfords, but I didn't care because I actually liked my comfortable shoes and still opt for comfort over style. I think pigeon toes are caused by hip dysplasia, which is considered suboptimal and which doctors like to treat by putting babies in casts.)

Our PE teachers told us we could not wear the same shoes for gym and for personal use, so every girl had a pair she kept in her gym locker and dutifully washed every Saturday, along with the black shorts with a white stripe and the white snap front shirt with our name on the pocket in indelible ink. Somewhere along the line, the teachers insisted that we wear sneakers with big hunking thick soles.

If I thought it was trendy to wear colored sneakers, I could never have imagined what a few years would do to the sneaker industry. Sneakers had always been made of double-stitched canvas bonded to rubber soles, but that was to change drastically about the mid-'70s.

Sneakers were no longer only canvas. They came in vinyl and leather as well, with fancy decorations. I remember my mother examining the leather sneakers my nieces had brought from Baltimore during a visit, and with unconcealed disgust remarking that the point of tennashoes was that they could be washed.

Now sneakers are made out of a plethora of materials: canvas, vinyl, and leather, to be sure; but also mesh, satin, rubber, flannel—just about any material that takes a needle and thread. Hightops are worn by both males and females, and other styles now include clogs, wedge, ballet, and classic. Some even have lights in the soles that flash as one walks.

Sneakers are sometimes referred to by various generic names, such as plimsolls (for the Brits), tennies, and kicks. Frequently, they are named by function. There are trainers, cross trainers, circuit trainers; running shoes, walking shoes, water shoes, athletic shoes; there are sneakers for hiking, trail running, aerobics, biking, skateboarding, and yes, playing tennis.

When I came across the term "skaters", I was confused. Were these the shoes that had retractable skate wheels embedded in the soles? That always seems dangerous to me, but lots of kids have them. No, these were shoes especially made for skateboarders, probably so they can run fast when they are caught skating in areas that are clearly marked "No Skateboarding!"

Often, sneakers are not referred to either generically or by function, but by brand. Converse, Vans, Skechers, ASICS, Nikes, Adidas, Reeboks for example. These brands come and go in popularity seemingly independent of quality or style.

There are shoes named after sports celebrities, which are considered highly valuable and sometimes go for ten or twenty times what I pay for mine. There's a sort of cottage industry in purchasing designer sneakers and reselling them for a profit. There's also a lot of money to be made in decorating sneakers and selling them on eBay. People are not supposed to wear these shoes, just to own them.

For my part, I think tennashoes is a perfectly good name. It has tradition and longevity on its side. It is not beset by changes in fashion and is neither pretentious nor self-effacing. It rolls easily off the tongue and is understood by everyone.

So, "tennashoes" it is. T-E-N-N-A-S-H-O-E-S.

The House Laurie Bought
Art French

We called our first house "Sheldon Jackson's Museum" for that intrepid Presbyterian missionary known as "The Bishop of all the Beyond." After being named Commissioner for the Territory of Alaska by the United States government, Sheldon Jackson began building schools all over that vast land from Sitka in the south east panhandle to Point Barrow on the arctic slope. He arranged a cooperative effort among various denominations to supply the teachers for these schools. Of course, the denominational headquarters started churches also. The U.S. government paid to build the schools while the churches supplied the teachers. So much for the separation of church and state.

This first home after we were married was built before the turn of the 20th century on St. Lawrence Island, Alaska, in the Eskimo village of Gambell. It was named in memory of the very first missionaries who were drowned at sea returning to the Island from their first furlough. This first framed building sat amidst the round split walrus hide and whale bone frame Eskimo dwellings. When this building was torn down during our time on the Island, we discovered tundra grass insulation in the walls. Our bedroom was the converted coal bin.

From that historic structure we moved into the apartment attached to the new church building. I helped complete that new home by installing the interior walls. The third pastoral dwelling was in the village of Savoonga on the Island. This was another small apartment incorporated in the church building. By this time our family had grown to four with two beautiful daughters.

From Alaska we moved to the mountain village of Idyllwild in Southern California. Our home was the manse, the first church, which was located immediately adjacent to that church. We didn't seem to be able to get very far from the church building itself. This was a wonderful old mountain lodge-style home with a huge stone fireplace and wide knotty pine paneling. However, we got tired of being so available whenever anyone wanted to get into the church and started looking for another house.

Also, I asked the Session for a housing allowance not really expecting them to agree since we lived in a perfectly suitable dwelling. However, the elders surprised me by agreeing to my request and offering $100 a month in housing allowance. We were thrilled with the prospect, knowing the house we wanted. It was another wonderfully well-built mountain home with fireplace and knotty pine paneling. Best of all it was located on a quiet dead end street, perfect for our young children now numbering three.

This house was owned by Mr. McPherson, a wonderful craftsman, who was a longtime member of the church now living off the Hill in a nursing facility. I called their daughter, Ruth, who lived in Long Beach, explained that I wanted to rent her parents' home but only had $100 a month in housing allowance from the church. She readily agreed.

Enter Laurie Morwood-Clark. He was a local realtor who also was the lay reader for the Episcopal fellowship. I had asked Laurie if I should have some kind of rental agreement being such a greenhorn regarding such matters.

Laurie took it from there in his usual efficient English manner. He drew up an agreement which laid out our monthly rental obligation. Then he added a clause which stated that after two years I had the right to buy the property. I, of course, said there was no way I was going to buy that property. That was the farthest thing from my mind. One didn't disagree with Laurie easily. He didn't suffer fools either. It was the proper thing to do even though we had no plans to leave Idyllwild. But two years seemed like a long way off, so I acquiesced.

About a year after we had moved to Lower Pine Crest Road, I began noticing strangers appearing in Sunday morning worship. This was unusual since few strangers came to worship except in the summer. Turned out to be a pastoral search committee from off the Hill. After three such visits and a candidating weekend, the Frenches were ready to move to Gardena, California.

Enter Mr. Morwood-Clark again who announced, "Now you're going to buy this house." To which I responded that was the silliest thing I had ever heard. We were moving away. Why would I purchase this property? Laurie's logic was as impeccable as he was. "You have two years' worth of payments invested in that place. That fulfills your down payment obligation. Of course, you're going to buy it." Ruth was in agreement again. So, of course, we bought the place against my better judgement, and we moved out. However, we had to rent it to help make the payments. Big mistake. After losing money, we decided to sell. The house didn't sell and we took it off the market. I got a call in Gardena one night from Idyllwild. It was Tony Tristano, whom I knew but not well. He wanted to buy the house and knew how to get the paper work done through the bank, so would not have to pay a realtor.

To back up: we had moved into the manse belonging to the First Presbyterian church of Gardena, California. After several years trying to work with an ineffective Manse Committee, we decided to move. Again we asked for housing allowance and were given the OK. It was about this time we decided to sell the Idyllwild property. The sale was consummated and the $10,000 profit was in the bank.

After deciding to vacate the Gardena manse we went house hunting and found the perfect house, we thought, in Gardena. We made an offer. However, the owner decided not to sell and took it off the market. We began looking again and found the exact same house in Torrance. Because it was in another city with a better reputation, it would cost $3,000 more. It was a spec house and in not nearly as good condition as the other house we wanted. Still we decided to purchase it. The four bedrooms were perfect for our family. Besides this location was within walking distance to the grade school, high school and El Camino College.

Best of all the $10,000 in the bank from the Idyllwild house that Laurie bought was just about enough for the down payment on the Torrance house with a few hundred dollars which we could afford to add. It meant we did not need to negotiate a loan from the church to make the purchase. What a gift Laurie had given us.

The sale of the Torrance house provided the money with which we remodeled our Monte Vista Grove apartment.

Thank you, Laurie.

LICE…Not Again!
Hedy Lodwick

This story came into being with accounts from two children and a granddaughter

I was startled when the following e-mail came from son Philip. He wrote:

"At 2:00 my cell phone rang with a call from the Poplar Bridge (school) Nurse. Amelia had lice and we needed to pick her up. Kathy canceled her patients while I made an appointment at Minnesota Lice Lady. We all met there at 3:00. Kathy and Ben checked out negative. They did not even want to check me. What? I still have a few strands of hair. Two hours and two hundred dollars later Amelia is lice free."

Goodness, now they have lice ladies! I had never heard of them nor about lice being so serious that parents had to be summoned from work to pick up their children. No doubt it was a school nurse who came to our class when I was in grade school and had us bend heads over our desks so she could check our hair. One slender girl with stringy dark hair had THEM. We all considered this girl rather dirty. Now she had LICE! Poor girl!

It wasn't from her because it was during summer vacation, but now I had lice! Brother Roland and I were preparing to travel to New Jersey with Mother to visit Uncle Hans and Aunt Sylvia. Grossmama was already there as she spent her summer months with them where it was cooler than with us in Maryland. We were to spend a few weeks and then return with her when summer was over. Mother didn't see anything in my hair when I complained of itching and she shrugged off the itching between my fingers also. She was busy ironing and packing and my complaints must have been an annoyance. I had been playing in the side yard and had pulled green weeds to decorate my mud pie display on the brick wall by our driveway. Alas, poison ivy!!! I know of no explanation for the lice. However, by the time we arrived in New Jersey, my Aunt was faced with a very sick little girl who had poison ivy *and* lice. The itching between the fingers had troubled me and I had tried to relieve it by chewing on them…giving me poison ivy inside and out. A doctor was summoned. He gave prescriptions for poison ivy and lice. Thankfully, I got well. However, Mother had returned to Maryland quickly to be with Dad, and Aunt Sylvia had the nasty job of helping me be rid of lice and treating poison ivy. She was not too pleased! I have always been sad remembering the vacation that should have been pure delight as the unfortunate summer with poison ivy and lice. After that, there were no lice stories until the summer of 1963.

That summer, our family was traveling from Egypt for home assignment. We lived in Cairo while in language study and while my husband, Bob, was working on an important assignment with the schools and colleges. This summer period corresponded to the time Mother's parents in Basel, Switzerland were celebrating their 60th wedding anniversary. We took daughter Marion out of first grade early and she and I flew to Basel to help celebrate. Our other daughter, Margaret, had missed too much school that year so she and Bob joined us later. When they arrived, Margaret's head was itching! They had been to a village before leaving and I checked for lice then but I had no idea how hard they were to see. We stopped off in London on the way to Boston where we arrived to visit Bob's sister. In London, I finally saw the nasty little critters (I wonder how many were shed in the airplane for someone else to collect?).

I was embarrassed when I told sister Peggy why we needed to buy lice killer. At the pharmacy, however, it was no problem. The needed shampoo was on the front shelf. "Follow the instructions on the bottle", we were told and all would be well. We did this and laundered sheets and left Boston lice free. It hadn't been an easy task, as Margaret's long braids had called for considerable time with the nit combs.

The next family encounter with lice was when Lisa Joy, our high school age granddaughter, wrote an account of *her* experience for the Bismarck newspaper. She had a regular column in the paper during her senior year. At that time, she planned to major in print journalism. The banner headline of this particular piece declared *"Getting lice at age 17? Now that's embarrassing."* She began by writing *"My family now owns a set of professional lice combs. What I want to know is who picks lice out of people's hair for a living? My Mom could. She's good at it."* She also confessed that *"My first concern was making sure no one outside my family found out. Even though I had a mild case, lice are right up there with chicken pox, pink eye, and leprosy when it comes to making people stay away."* She then continued for several columns telling all the effort necessary to banish the critters. In conclusion she wrote," *It was just lice, an annoyance, as my Mom said. It's gone now and someday if my kids get lice, I'll know exactly what to do: call my Mom"*

Well, my aunt, I, and daughters Margaret and Marion were the lice ladies of our day. Now it seems it has indeed become a profession. When I wondered about this to Philip, he replied writing *"They say … lice have started to become immune to that "bottle of stuff"…. You can do it yourself, but it takes lots of patience and if you are not experienced you probably will not get it right the first time. I guess there is enough of a problem that it can be a pretty good business in metro areas. The place we went to was started by a woman who volunteered at her girls' school and people offered to pay her. She now has a salon with 10 technicians…. Kathy had checked last night but did not realize …what she was seeing were the nits."*

Daughter Marion added what she learned from her own experience and that of her friends. *"Oh yes, I've known about Lice Ladies for a while. Marly and I did Sophie's hair when she was a teen. Hours checking her hair, strand by strand, in my backyard-…. Friend, Cynde, has taken care of her own girls. Three thick heads of hair to search…. mountains of laundry with three girls sharing everything. She gets a bit crazed! But friend Debbie just packs daughter Melanie up in the car, heads to Seattle (about 5 hours round trip) and heads to the Lice Ladies. They've had her hair done there at least twice. A couple hours and a couple hundred dollars later, hair is lice free, pampered and conditioned. For Cynde & Randy, with three girls…. not possible to indulge for that kind of money, so it's the old fashioned way. At Opepo (the preschool Jacob attended)… there were periodic outbreaks and crackdowns….no stuffed animals, hair in braids….but neither Jacob or Justin ever got the critters. I mistakenly shampooed the whole family when I was young and did not know better. During one of the outbreaks at Opepo, I searched the boys' hair and was just about done when I found a tiny bug… I had it on my finger and was examining it when it jumped. It was late, but I sent David to the grocery for lice shampoo. Washed everybody's hair, changed sheets and such… only to discover LICE DON'T JUMP! It was probably a flea."*

And so ends our family's education about lice and lice ladies then and now!

We Had Everything But Money
Margy Wentz

Chronicle of a remarkable era in our history – the Great Depression. The story of a remarkable generation of people born just about the time the 20th century began, somewhere between the presidencies of McKinley and Teddy Roosevelt.

We are the sons and daughters, grandchildren, and great-grandchildren.

It was their fate to be afflicted by wars, plagues, famines, epidemics, droughts and floods of near- Old Testament proportions. Yet they did much more than survive. They stubbornly and bravely endured, sustained by their Bible, their patriotism, and their determination that things could be made better than they were.

Theirs was the generation that went from outhouses to outer space, from kerosene lamps to computers, from straw mattresses to supersonic jets.

They made do during the bad times and adjusted to monumental changes in the world around them. They persevered through it all, anchoring their happiness and fulfillment on the belief that family was what mattered most.

They marched away to fight in World War I, the war to end all wars. What it turned out to be was a barbaric battle of rat=filled trenches, poison gas and perpetual mud that shattered minds as well as bodies. More than 116,000 Americans died and another 204,000 were wounded—many to live out their maimed lives in veterans/ hospitals.

So Johnny came marching home and married the girl he left behind and started a family and settled down to earn a living. And just about the time things seemed to be going pretty well, the Great Depression hit.

Soon 35% of all Americans were out of work. Banks closed. Insurance companies failed. Businesses locked their doors. The great droughts of 1934 and 1936 burned out the heartland, and entire states were turned into the Dust Bowl. It was "Hard Times".

. . .incredible changes—the first automobiles, a telephone in the house, electricity, radio, running water, refrigeration, extermination of diphtheria, polio, heart transplants, travel by air, television, and prosperity. Our family enjoyed the accommodation but we enjoyed most who we were as family and our community bound together in life's journey.

From the Bottom of the Trunk
Hedy Lodwick

When I was growing up, it was a seasonal ritual. There was not enough closet space to keep winter <u>and</u> summer things hanging, so-out-of-season things were stored in our trunk. As we grew, we had to try clothes on for size, but more fun was trying on the special things mother kept in the trunk. There was Dad's swallow-tailed tux which he wore to the opera when a student in Germany. There was Grossmama's Salvation Army bonnet. I wish I had these still, but Mother was not a saver and she surely didn't know what to do with them after Grossmama and Dad died. Where she sent them, I do not know.

Because my husband Bob and I packed trunks when we traveled overseas, these served us well then also. When we moved to New Jersey with an infant son, we covered one trunk to use as a changing table in his room. I can't remember where we placed our trunks in other places, but I do know that for years we stored many keepsakes in the bottom. Today we have only one trunk, kept in the corner of our bedroom. On it I store boxes of pictures waiting for attention. Moving all this when I want to get out our sweaters, our winter bedspread, and the purses I need with darker clothes is something of an ordeal. A few weeks ago, I was about to close it up again when our writing teacher asked "Have you saved a special outfit from your youth? What was it? Why did you save it?" Well, it was not just a special outfit but lots of the pictures I had drawn in high school, some of them large-size pastels. Also, there are special posters from World Council Assemblies and such. Why we have kept them I do not know. The pictures speak of a time when I debated going to art school after High School or to a Presbyterian College and then to Seminary. Obviously I chose the latter and from time to time, I wonder what life might have been like on the path not taken. Certainly the path taken has been full, challenging, and wonderful in its own mysterious ways. Anyway, the pictures are there and Marion was quite taken by them when she helped me with the trunk opening for the past Spring season.

At the bottom of the trunk now is my wedding dress. It's a wrinkled heap of Dotted Swiss which I would have dispatched long ago, but Bob always wanted me to keep it and now so does Marion. So, it keeps going back to the bottom. Another well-worn item is a quilt Bob's grandmother made for his bed when he was little. It has squares with little bonnet clad boys and girls. It is a well-known pattern, I believe. It is also too worn for use, but I always fancied myself cutting out better squares and making pillows of them. I've been thinking that for years and now our children are grown and so are our grandchildren and my sewing machine stands idle. So this relic keeps returning to the trunk bottom – for some future generation to discard? Actually, it is on the bottom of the cedar chest. Since the question was raised, I have saved out a few of the trunk bottom items. One is a sampler that I believe was embroidered in 7th grade Home Economics (Goodness, they still seemed to think girls should know how to embroider back then!) We were to show how to use the different stitches. At one time, this sampler must have been framed, but it is certainly not the delicate thing one sometimes sees from earlier generations. Another item, this time from a high school art class, is one panel of some curtains which I had stenciled. These were put to use but why I have this one panel now, I do not know. I suppose next spring, it will return to the bottom of the trunk.

Another piece of clothing is the romper suit that was Bob's when he was little. What impractical garments little children wore then! If I remember correctly, we once had two of these. What happened to the other one, I do not know.

We saved some of our own children's outfits, which I found darling at the time. The girls had little lawn dresses delicately embroidered in the Philippines. They had to be ironed after washing! Oh my. What a chore for busy moms. After a time, I packed up sample outfits as well as the blankets knit by my Mother, for each of our children. I believe they did not use these since the much-easier-to-use outfits went in and out of the drier with no ironing – or hand washing. Are any of these saved today? I do not know........

Why do we save such things? Again, I do not know. Sentiment perhaps, or not wanting to let go of precious memories from childhood and youth.

One garment I have saved was given to me by a British mother who lost her soldier son (or perhaps sailor) while he was in the hospital in Dunkerque. Bob had been the English speaking pastor who had been with him and then could conduct the funeral. I came along for the service and the young man's mother could not help but notice that I was very pregnant. She asked me then if she could send me her son's baby garments she had been keeping for future grandchildren. Of course, I said she could.

In time, I took a picture of Marion wrapped in one of these "woolies". I have kept only one of them. It is a souvenir of a young man we never knew and of a mother's sorrow and dashed dream of a future with grandchildren. Somehow, I have not been able to let it go, and this, too, will find its way to the trunk bottom for our children to do with as they like, once we are gone.

Twice Blessed with Harold Reginald Ray
and Frederick Leonard Bayford
Gloria Shamblin

I never met my father, Harold, and have often wished that I could have spent a day or even an hour with him. He knew my mother was pregnant before he died, but he didn't know I was a girl. I have been told I look like him. Most of my family is blonde and blue eyed; with my brown eyes and dark hair, I take after his side of the family. He was the youngest son in a family of six and the earliest picture I have of him is in a dress on the nanny's knee. He grew up to be tall, and as a typical air force man of the 1940s had a short back and side's hairstyle and an Errol Flynn moustache. By all accounts he was a smart dresser, when in civvies (civilian clothes) and expected my mother to be the same way, which she continued until she died at 96. His career as an accountant was cut short by the war. According to his sisters he could do no wrong and I have always thought this was something I had to live up to. My mother and his youngest sister were in kindergarten together and since they remained friends until my mother died. Auntie Kay said that dad said he would marry my mother as early as elementary school.

As an adult I was to meet a cousin, who as a 12-year-old had spent the night with my father before his last flight. They played checkers and talked of Wooster and Jeeves. I inherited his taste for board games and books. Several years ago my mother gave me her engagement ring, and along with a few photographs it is one of the few tangible mementoes that I own. Wearing the ring gives me a link with both parents.

I remember when my mother started dating my dad, Fred. She had one dashing young suitor that knew the way to a widow's heart was through gifts to her young daughter. Alas, for me as a 5-year-old girl, I had no choice in my mother's marriage partner. Fred Bayford was an insurance man that would come to our home to collect six-penny premiums. Our home at that time, in Sidcup Kent, was with an aunt, uncle and their two preteen children. My mother offered to sew a button on the insurance man's blue striped demob suit and the rest is history. I did not like this man with grey hair that wanted to put his hand in mine. My mother could hold my hand and no one else, but since I was a very obedient child, I did not dare to say how I felt.

They were soon married, a very quiet affair with no children in attendance. Quite soon we moved out of London into "digs" in a beach town called Bognor Regis. This was the start of my life with my new dad. In retrospect, this man loved me unconditionally; there was never any step-parent in our relationship. He was soon to call me Whiskas. I eventually found out this was short for "cat's whiskers" which meant that you owned an early kind of radio that was powered by Cat's Whiskers, in which case you were very special. To this day my mother uses many wartime expressions that I finally understand, her favourite being "half a jif."

Dad taught me how to swim in the sea; he had a moth-eaten prewar black wool swim suit. My swimming costume was one of the early bubbly nylon varieties. We would go down to the beach early morning or early evening, get into a calm sea and he would hold the palm of his hand under my chin and teach me breast stroke.

Often I would jump on the back of his motor bike and he would take me to school. I would have one hand around him and the other clutching my school beret so it would not fall off. None of the other primary school children were picked up by a dad on a motorcycle. He loved to clean my brown, beetle crusher school shoes. The cloth was old underwear, the polish ox blood and you could always pick me out in school line up in my smart school gymslip, I was the one with shiny maroon shoes.

He could help me with my French and arithmetic in elementary school. Being positive was his nature, he beamed rather than smiled. He never wore shorts or sandals and would mow the lawn in a sports jacket, sometimes wearing a cravat instead of a tie. Everyone was treated the same whatever their station in life. Whether with Lords or ordinary people, he seemed to fit in anywhere. This was a big lesson to me. Over his lifetime he had many jobs to support our family and he never complained. He became very well known in our town for his kindness. Sometimes he would come home with a picture or a punnet of strawberries as payment for an odd job he had done. In those days our family did not close sentences with I love you, but we knew they had that feeling in their hearts. In later years after I moved to Pasadena, he was always there at Gatwick airport to meet me. He died suddenly at 84, the afternoon of one of his work days.

I had a difficult time at the airport when I flew back and he was not there. I helped write his obituary, it was simple; he was an extraordinary, ordinary man with the helping hands. A long way from when I would not let him hold mine.

Although they never met, both my father and my dad loved my mother and I felt they could have been good friends.

PAIN is
Martin Miller-Hessel

The San Francisco Giants won a tightly played World Series last night in Game VII against the greatly disappointed Kansas City Royals. I was delighted for my wife, Pam's, home town team. I was aware of the Royals' pain. Athletes know about pain, both physical and emotional.

I am not much of an athlete, but not for lack of trying. I don't have natural eye-motor skill coordination. But I finally found a nitch running 10 K races and jogging daily during my middle years.

The first real sports adventure I remember involved roller-skating on top of heavy wood church tables. My older brother, Gene, and others lined the tables up in the low-ceilinged social hall of Ellinwood-Malate Church in Manila where neighborhood children often played during long, humid and hot tropical evenings. I was six; Gene (I always called him Genie then) was 12.

We strapped on the old fashioned skates (using a skate key to tighten the front grips). Gene and his friends began rolling around on the table tops, deftly stopping before the edge or, after a brief flight, landing smoothly on the tiled floor surface below.

It looked like so much fun. I ran back to our manse, grabbed my skates and came back to join in the robust fun. When Gene wasn't watching I managed to scramble up onto a table and start rolling.

I rolled right off the far end, coming down hard on my chin, and created an instant puddle of blood from the resulting cut.

My parents were promptly notified (perhaps by my howling cries, or by my brother). He may have tried to staunch the bleeding, like the surgeon he would one day become.

I was rushed to the small clinic of our family physician (and faithful congregant) Dr. Joe (Jose) Reyes. Mom described how terrified I was of the anticipated pain from an anesthesia shot and stitches. I was a scrawny little guy, but I put up much loud, sweaty and squirmy resistance to all the help our good and loving doctor was trying to administer. It took every adult available to pin me down. Quickly, Dr. Joe performed a smooth repair: "So he won't be disfigured when he grows up," he said.

I survived. The pain was no fun, but it wasn't as bad as I clearly expected. One can barely find the fine scar line well under my chin today.

Pain simply is. It comes with our admission ticket to life.

A few more encounters with physical and emotional pain in childhood and youth, prepared me for the more difficult adult experiences we all pass through. But I still feel sorry for those sad and shocked-looking Royals; and, I never tried to roller-skate on a table of any kind again.

Unstoppable Climber
Carolyn French

It has always been interesting to me how babies demonstrate certain behavioral characteristics at a very young age, which often persist through their lives. Our youngest daughter, Leslie, is a case in point. Once she was walking, she was climbing - always raring to go.

At age 3, she fearlessly climbed the ladders of the pueblos at Mesa Verde. In June of 1969 at age five, she delighted in climbing in and out of the opening in pew backs at the Presbyterian Church of Gardena, California while Art preached his candidating sermon for the position as Pastor of the congregation.

The next summer, we exchanged houses for a week with friends from Idyllwild. Venturing on a tricycle where she shouldn't have been, she flipped over a barbed wire fence, resulting in cuts on her face near her ears, and the front of her neck. Also she had a nasty long cut from her mid-thigh to three inches below the knee, resulting in 39 stitches altogether plus a tetanus shot!

In fourth grade her prowess was monkey bars, but one day she missed a bar just as the bell rang to return to class. She landed on her wrist severing both the ulna and radius. To align and set the bones, an axillary block and overnight stay in the hospital were required.

When it came to choosing a church camp in Junior High, the decision was easy for Leslie to decide: backpacking with "Uncle Jim." Each of the campers carried 40-50 pound backpacks. "Uncle Jim" was a beloved leader, trail blazer and mentor for many teenagers.

After living, going to college, and working in Connecticut for ten years, Leslie moved back west settling in Sunnyvale, California and working in computer technology at Lotus Development Corporation. While working there, Jamie Clark, who had been supported by their corporation for his successful attempt to summit Mt. Everest, came to speak about his experiences on that difficult trek. He shared his conviction that "Beyond fear is freedom." Jamie Clarke's sharing really captivated Leslie and since the company provided a month's sabbatical to employees in the sixth year of employment she qualified for the time off. Thus, she arranged to go on the trek to the base camp of Mount Everest with Jamie and his wife Barbara in April 1999.

When Leslie told us of her plans, I thought to myself "Oh, my gosh Leslie, will you ever stop climbing?" We were quite concerned, but became increasingly supportive of her as we learned how detailed and carefully arranged the trip was. She had a probable but not exact write up of where they would be each day along the trip and we learned there were teahouses along the ascent that could be used for overnight (though she never elected to sleep in one, being satisfied with the usual tents). There was even a

Leslie and the trek leader Barbara in their Chupa dresses.

medical facility part way up the trail that had been built and was supported by the Edmond Hillary Foundation to give clinical care to the local people. The hikers were given lists of what medication they should carry in case of painful injury, allergies to bee stings or what have you. They were also given instructions regarding preparations, getting in shape physically and so on, which she diligently followed, often climbing in nearby mountains, breaking in the new hiking boots, working out at the gym, as well as all her other sports involvements which included snow and water skiing, mountain biking, volleyball, hiking, camping, etc. We also learned that the Sherpas took care of providing meals, putting up and taking down tents, and packing the supplies on yaks. Individually the hikers only carried day packs for personal and accessible needs during the day. Leslie later reported that she thought it was the easiest climbing trip she'd ever taken because the Sherpas did so much *for* them including bringing them warm tea/milk combination to drink first thing in the morning as well as a bowl of hot water for washing up. Amazingly, the entire trip, airfare and all, was about $3000 as opposed to over $100,000 dollars required for summiting Mt. Everest.

Soon after we got adapted to her planned excursion she said she planned to go to Thailand, flying to Krabi and taking a boat to Rai Leh for some rest and relaxation for one week after her Everest trip. There she planned to do some rock climbing and also learn scuba diving. Since she didn't know anyone going there at the same time, she would be on her own. I felt quite leery but then she learned that a couple from the Everest trek would be going to the same place in Thailand! What a relief!

When the time came to begin her sabbatical jaunt she flew to Bangkok and then on to Katmandu where the group spent three days acclimating to the altitude of 8000 feet. The plan was to take two weeks climbing up from Katmandu to the Base Camp at 17,500 feet, and then one week to return. She & leader Barbara each bought a Chupa (a type of wrap-around full length dress) like the native women wore. They also bought prayer flags to post along the way. To feel closer to her while she was away, I wrote to her every day, and gave her the notes and letters when she returned.

As it turned out, she had a wonderful week for the trip – it had been drier than usual, having only rained a couple times lightly. The climbers, per instructions, walked a slow steady pace, and that plus overnighting many places along the way, helped them to adapt well to the altitude. Only one in their party needed to turn back due to rather severe altitude sickness and some of the sherpas escorted him and his wife to lower altitude.

After reaching base camp at 17,500 foot level, those who wished, were invited to hike to Kala Patar which was 18,500 feet in order to get a better angle for photographing the peak as the moon arose. Of course Leslie chose to go! She took the prayer flags she had bought in Katmandu and strung them up, praying for peace in the world. She was even feeling well enough to go back up to that level to see the sun rise over the peak the next morning!

Leslie did well the whole trek until close to the halfway point on the way back down Everest, when she began feeling a bit out of sorts, so she was checked at the Kunde medical facility. Her blood pressure was elevated. Since she was descending they felt she'd do okay and just told her to have it rechecked at home. She did, and there has been no further problem.

Two days before Leslie left Rai Leh in Thailand, she took a scuba diving lesson. At the end of class as she and the leader were moving toward the shore, Leslie suddenly felt strange and very shaky. She and several in the class had been getting stung by jellyfish. The instructor, thinking Leslie was having a seizure, told her to lie back and she'd float her to the beach. A man walking along the shore and seeing this scenario, came to help saying he was a doctor from Germany! Meanwhile, the friends along on the trip, came over to find her, realized *she* was the one in trouble, and gave the doctor their anaphylactic kit to use. Leslie said she remembered "coming to" as he injected the epinephrine, but was still not able to verbally answer his questions for a while. The native workers at the place she was staying said they had never seen anyone with this reaction to the jellyfish in their waters. They brought leaves mixed with vinegar and sponged her leg with them. After several hours of that, along with the pain medication she had taken, she got relief.

When we met her at the airport in Los Angeles her leg looked like someone had whiplashed her from the knee to the ankle – with red stripes like a barber's pole. When she finally saw her own doctor, he told her she'd actually had a neurological rather than anaphylactic reaction from the jellyfish poison. She did fully recover, but not without itching keeping her awake many nights, even with soaking in cold water and applying a salve the doctor had ordered for relief.

Despite scars and broken bones, God certainly has provided for our daredevil daughter in ever so many ways, keeping her and now her husband, too, safe in their many adventures together, for they *both* are unstoppable climbers!

This Little Light of Mine
Tom Wentz

When I was ten years old, our family moved from Hogestown to a farm on Winding Hill Road, south of Mechanicsburg. Village life changed to rural life and a more individualized life style. My life transitioned from child play to boyhood activities with purpose: learning skills and experiencing cultural values. A ten-year-old tends to prefer light cultural values, but Dad leaned towards work skills. This is a memory of how our mutual interests influenced my growing up.

I think Dad's interest wasn't influenced as much by the Puritan "idle hands" problem, but more around the concept that all play and no work was un-American. I remember he entered into a contract with Ralston Purina Feeds to get 500 free chicks if we purchased their feed. Dad thought it would be good work for my brother and me to learn, as well as a money-maker. Five hundred pee-pees, and one half grew to be fryers and the other half capons. When the chickens became of age, there was a neighborhood canning event between the Wentz and Basehore families; we plucked, boiled, put into jars, and sealed some of those chickens for later consumption. I mention this because it introduces Sally Harris, the local interest editor for the Harrisburg Patriot News and a participant in the event.

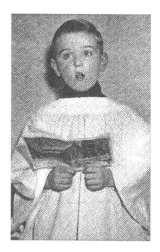

In the choir

Sally Harris heard kids singing at the piano, asked who a particular boy was, and that boy was me! She contacted the Director of Music at Market Square Presbyterian Church, the big church in Harrisburg, and I, without audition, joined the Children's Choir. You cannot imagine the good fortune. Most choir members were 6 to 12 years old. I was already 10, and my voice didn't change until I was 16. Prof. Miller solicited a member of the congregation to pay for lessons. I was a featured soloist when the offering was taken and for special musicals. I sang for Rotary, Optimist, Women's Christian Temperance Union, Presbyterian Women, Wednesday night services, the Presbyterian old folk's home, and the County Poor Farm, as well as became well indoctrinated with special attention and pot luck suppers. I was also the child soloist in Mendelssohn's dramatic oratorio, "Elijah." Some years back, I was managing a booth at the National Presbyterian General Assembly. Two ladies from Carlisle, PA came up to the booth and when I mentioned my name and that I had grown up in the Mechanicsburg area, they said, "O' little Tommy Wentz!"

Mother drove, my sister accompanied on the piano, and I sang. I learned one could have a natural talent, but if one did not have a presence with one's audience, that talent would be hidden under a bushel, where the light shines dimly. My voice was a natural gift to be trained, but presentation was a creative relationship. In ministry, talent and knowledge are important, but honest relationships are essential. My experiences in singing and music instilled my appreciation for the arts.

A piece of this little light of mine.

Elijah

UNDER THE STEEPLE

How the Church I Served in Chicago Started
Masaya Hibino

For twenty-four years, from September 1966 to July 1990, I served as pastor of Church of Christ, Presbyterian in the North Side of Chicago near Wrigley Field. The reason I am writing this is that this church had its beginning through the grace of God and is an amazing demonstration of sacrificial love and commitment of the leaders of Chicago's Fourth Presbyterian Church during World War II.

I was called to serve the Church of Christ, Presbyterian in 1966, twenty-four years after the following dramatic story. The church still had nearly 50 or 60 members in the congregation who had personal experiences with the love and sacrifice of the Fourth Presbyterian Church. We had newspaper articles from that period, and some church records. I was able to contact and correspond with Dr. John M. Mulder, former president of Louisville Presbyterian Seminary. John was brought up in the Fourth Church and his father had served as the Clerk of Session for many years including during World War II.

Before World War II, I was told that there were some 500 Japanese and Japanese-Americans living in Chicago. Some of these Nikkei (persons of Japanese ancestry) became Christians and formed a small Japanese speaking congregation under Pastor Ai Chi Tsai, a Formosan pastor who was fluent in Japanese language. They worshipped in a church in Hyde Park on Chicago's South Side, but when World War II started, this small Japanese congregation was expelled from the meeting place. They thought, they could meet in the homes of church members. However, the terms of the Alien Enemy Registration Act of 1940 prohibited assembly of more than three Japanese people (other than family members inside their homes), because it could be considered subversive to the U.S. war effort. They were allowed to worship in a Christian church building, but the congregation did not own any church building, and they lacked financial resources to buy or to build one.

These Nikkei Christians approached a number of Protestant churches in the city for worship space, but most of the Christian churches considered it unpatriotic to accept Japanese Christians. Those churches turned down their requests.

Finally, this small Japanese group approached the prominent Fourth Presbyterian Church, which was the largest Presbyterian church in Chicago and a leading Protestant congregation in the city. Set in a gothic revival cathedral building designed by architect Ralph Adams Cram and adorned with beautiful stained-glass windows, the Fourth is located on North Michigan Avenue in the middle of what is now known as the Magnificent Mile, a high-end shopping district. The church, in accordance with Presbyterian rules, planned to consider the request of the Japanese congregation in its session meeting. This was at the start of World War II, and Nikkeis were being treated as enemies of the United States. Somehow, news was leaked to the public that the Fourth Church was going to consider opening its door to a small Japanese-speaking congregation. The church office began to receive threatening phone calls: "open the doors to the Japanese Christians, and we will destroy your stained glass windows and damage your property."

The Senior Pastor, Harrison Ray Anderson, fully favored opening the doors of the church. Anderson referred the request to a special committee of the session, which unanimously recommended that the Japanese congregation be allowed to worship in the church. Then "a violent and emotional debate erupted; the horrible passions stirred by the war arose in the arguments," wrote Dr. John M. Mulder. The three-man special committee included his father, John Mulder, who had served as clerk of session for many years and his godfather, Dr. Stewart Thomson." Godfather is not usually used in Presbyterian tradition, but John M. used that term in his correspondence to me. "At one point my godfather threatened to resign from the session and leave the church if the session failed to sustain the committee's recommendation," Mulder wrote.

The session adjourned without reaching any decision. When it reconvened a week later, Dr. Mulder wrote in an April 2013 letter to me, his father was asked by Dr. Anderson to listen to the debate. At a certain point in the meeting, his father "sensed that there was majority" and signaled the moderator to take the vote. What was the result? The session accepted the recommendation of the special committee by a one vote majority. Just one vote! Without that one vote, there would have been no Church of Christ, Presbyterian (Japanese-American Church) in Chicago. Dr. Harrison Ray Anderson informed the Session's decision to the Mayor of Chicago, the police commissioner, and the FBI to assure the Japanese Christians refuge in Fourth Presbyterian Church.

In May 1942, the Church first opened the small but adequately-sized Timothy Stone Chapel to the Japanese congregation. "Not an eye was dry, and many women wept openly when we gathered in Fourth Church the first time and Dr. Anderson welcomed us," Harry K. Shigeta, a commercial photographer, wrote of that experience. Dr. Anderson, wearing his clerical robe, stood at the church door every Sunday and welcomed Japanese Christians to worship by shaking hands with them. At the end of their worship, he would stand at the door again and make sure that each worshipper would be able to safely leave the church. Chicago winters can be brutally cold, especially on Michigan Avenue with its proximity to the lake. It took a deep Christian love to do what Dr. Anderson did, not only one time, but continually until the end of the war. One Issei (first generation) elder, Akira Soraoka of Church of Christ, Presbyterian was never able to share his experience without teary eyes.

It was courageous for the Fourth Presbyterian Church to do what it did in that historical context and to risk possible vandalism to its exquisite building. There were at least a few hundred churches representing protestant denominations in Chicago at that time, but it was only Fourth Presbyterian Church that stepped forward by faith and love to open the door.

During the War, nearly 30,000 Nikkei moved to Chicago from the concentration camps in California, Arizona, Arkansas, Colorado and Utah. They were prohibited to return to the West Coast during the war but were allowed to move inland to northern cities, such as Chicago, Cleveland and Cincinnati. Cities were looking for workers and Chicago, in particular, welcomed Japanese workers, who proved reliable and well-educated. There were a number of Christians among Nikkeis who moved to Chicago, and they also sought a place to worship. The only church opened to them was the Fourth Church. As the number of worshippers increased, Timothy Stone Chapel quickly became too small. The Fourth opened the medium-sized Westminster Chapel which could accommodate 300. Even that became too small as worshippers increased.

Among the worshippers were pastors from various denominations including Baptist, Congregational, Free Methodist, Methodist, and Holiness denominational churches from the West Coast. After the war, those pastors started their own denominational churches and pulled members out from the congregation that was meeting at the Fourth Presbyterian Church.

Those who remained at the Fourth Church continued to worship there until 1953. By then, they had saved enough money to put a down payment on a church building of their own. Chicago Presbytery approved the congregation as a member church and its purchase of the Lakeview Evangelical Free Church's building on Sheffield Avenue near Wrigley Field. The first worship service at their new building took place on Sunday, July 15, 1953.

On the last Sunday at Fourth Church, the Japanese congregation, in appreciation for the love and support of the Fourth Church, presented a monetary gift to Dr. Harrison Ray Anderson. According to Dr. John M. Mulder, Dr. Anderson traveled to Scotland and the island of Iona where he purchased several small silver Celtic crosses with this money. He presented one cross to the moderator of the Presbyterian Church in the United States of America (PCUSA), and another to the Presbyterian Church in the United States (PCUS) which was also known as Southern Presbyterian Church. Later, he presented a third cross to the moderator of the United Presbyterian Church in North America (UPCNA). "In making the presentations, he expressed the hope that someday these three crosses would be welded together as one," Mulder writes.

The crosses became the symbol of the moderator's office. When the UPCNA and the PCUSA merged in 1958, two of the crosses were bound together. Mulder says, "In a dramatic moment in Atlanta in 1983, an Asian jeweler—with hands trembling—welded the three crosses together on the platform of the General Assembly in front of more than five thousand

Presbyterians." Twice I have seen the three-in-one forged cross, carried by two moderators of our General Assembly, when each visited Monte Vista Grove Homes in Pasadena, where I now live. Knowing the histories of the crosses and having had a part in the ministry of the Church of Christ, Presbyterian in Chicago, I had a special feeling of gratitude to God.

Dr. Harrison Ray Anderson passed away in 1979 at the age of 86 in Santa Barbara, California. One of his memorial services was held at Fourth Presbyterian Church in Chicago. It was my honor to be invited as a participant in the service and to remember the important part Dr. Anderson had in helping to start the Church of Christ, Presbyterian in Chicago, where I was privileged to serve for twenty-four years.

Only one vote! I thank God for the members of the session who voted to open the Fourth Church to a Japanese Christian Church in the face of public opposition. Only one vote majority determined the Christian ministry of the Japanese-American church in Chicago!

A Lively Church
Norman E. Thomas

In 2005 I attended the World Council of Churches' Conference on World Mission and Evangelism in Athens, Greece. Leaders of churches in greater Athens invited conference-goers to participate in Sunday worship with them. I chose to go to Saint Marina, a Greek Orthodox church in the city. The climb up the Hill of the Nymphs to the church provides a spectacular view of the Acropolis upon a nearby hill.

A priest, who attended the Conference, informed me that the worship liturgy would last for three hours from 7 to 10 a.m. He advised me to come a bit late for the service. Upon arrival I found that I, at age 73, was one of the younger persons present. A woman veiled and dressed all in black, and her family members and friends, sat in the row in front of me. At the time of prayers and intercessions, the priests and others gathered around her. It was the 40th day after the death of her husband, the day when there would be special prayers for her and other mourners in the Sunday service.

I participated in the liturgy sung by the priests and their assistants. Before each major part of the service — the readings from the epistles and gospels and the Eucharist — the priests and their assistants processed around the church with crosses and icons.

Is this just a church for older folks? I wondered. Back in the United States I had taught for twenty-five years about the dynamics of church renewal. In my home state of New Hampshire, for example, one can see in town after town closed church buildings that now are libraries, or playhouses, or even antique shops. Many served worshipping congregations for less than a century. Where the children did not catch the faith of their parents, those churches closed after the deaths of their elderly members. I taught that every local church is potentially within one generation of extinction.

About 9:30 a.m. some families with children arrived for worship. Soon the worshipping congregation more than doubled in size. The young families arrived just in time for the Eucharist. To my surprise not all worshippers received the sacrament of bread and wine. Instead, it was given primarily to children and their parents. The priest gave special attention to the one to two year-olds who had recently been baptized. With care he placed a spoonful of bread soaked in wine into each young mouth.

With enthusiasm we all got to sing a hymn at the close of the liturgy. After the benediction the children came forward first, followed by the adults, to consume the bread that remained at the church altar. Their conversation with laughter animated the space.

Saint Marina Church

While the children went to Sunday school, I remained with other visitors to take a tour of St. Marina's and learn more about their ministries. The church building is beautiful. Built in the 1920s in the Byzantine style, it has a central dome and four transepts (side aisles). A famous painter decorated the walls with frescoes in a distinctive style from Central Europe. Among the icons is one to Saint Marina for whom the church is named. She is believed to have died as a martyr in 304 CE in her home town of Antioch (now the location of the modern-day city of Pisidia in Turkey). All Orthodox churches celebrate July 17th each year as Saint Marina's day.

Of course, the site of Saint Marina Church predates the Christian era. Archeologists found evidence that a pagan shrine was on this site as early as the 6th century BCE. Here water bubbled up out of the rock that was believed to have healing powers. Expectant mothers, and those with sick babies, came here to pray for safe labor and for healing of children.

In the 4th century, after Emperor Constantine became a Christian, Christians began to worship on this site. The modern church contains within it a natural 13th century cave church. It is now the site of the church baptistery.

After lunch I saw families arriving dressed in their finery as if for a wedding. Instead, it was for the baptism of twin boys. Their godmother, who was to make a life commitment to care for them, was given a place of special honor. The twins had just celebrated their first birthdays—the desired age for Orthodox baptisms. In the ceremony the priest took each boy in turn, who had been undressed for the ceremony, and immersed him three times in the font in the name of God the Father, Son, and Holy Spirit.

This natural 13th century cave church is now used as a baptistery

Saint Marina is a seven-day a week church. Yes, they offer daily worship but much more. Each day they serve a meal to the needy (as do other Orthodox churches in Athens, who together serve 2,500 meals a day). The priests shared that an average of 2-3 persons daily come, ask for, and receive financial assistance. The parish also provides housing for five elderly women.

I left Saint Marina that Sunday with a new appreciation of the Orthodox approach to mission and ministry. Here there has been continuity in proclamation of the faith over more than 1,500 years. That's sixty generations! The Orthodox believe that the church's mission is the Eucharist, but more. It is expressed as the Holy Spirit works in the lives of faithful believers seven days a week. It begins with the special caring that I observed in worship for both the young children and the grieving widow. I felt blessed to have been welcomed by such a lively church.

The Day of the Ingenious Ruse in Apple Valley
Bill Hansen

It was Friday and the church was swarming with Fall Rummage Sale customers. They had lined up that morning behind the ropes that enclosed the church yard. It was no small enterprise. The two events, the Spring and Fall rummage sales, reaped $40,000 dollars each year to add to the missionary outreach of the Church of the Valley congregation.

In addition to that the Rummage Sale was a major time of fellowship for the participants in the Voyagers Group whose members were all of retirement age. They comprised an enthusiastic ministry of 100 and more retirees. For the three days and nights of the sale they brought their motor homes and campers to the church grounds for an encampment. They shared meals prepared by a special crew in the church dining room, eat in shifts and work through the day at their stations. Some Voyagers returned home at the end of the day, but many remain to enjoy the evenings relaxing together outside and reflecting on the day's experiences.

The necessary collecting, storing, sorting, pricing, displaying of the goods to be sold at the Sale was an all-year-long project. The opening day of the Sale had a carnival-like atmosphere with customers lined up surrounding the church premises. A hundred or more people waited behind the ropes and then after the workers gathered for prayer, the ropes were dropped and the signal given for the sale to begin. Then it became like a re-enactment of the Oklahoma Land Rush as the eager customers came flying, leaping over furniture, scrambling to reach their favorite items, good naturedly pushing through the doors to reach the clothing and jewelry and gift departments inside the Family Life Center and adjacent rooms.

It was one year on the first Friday of one of the Sales that a small crew was together in the adjacent Fellowship Hall assembling and folding bulletins for that Sunday's worship service. Paul Alfred, the Staff member for Outreach Ministries, was assigned to the Big Items Department of the sale. Paul had promised to pitch in to help fold bulletins for the Sunday service. It was a skeleton crew because of the Sale. Paul was late arriving to fold the bulletins because he was tied up with a transaction. Every year there were Big items that were contributed for the Sale. That year a member had donated his mint condition, classic 1960's, Lincoln Continental with only 35,000 miles on it. It was the classic model with a rear enclosed mount for the spare tire which was designated as the Continental Kit. It added to the worth of the car and the car itself was a beauty!!! Paul had been out on a drive demonstrating the Lincoln Continental to a prospective buyer. But he was back now after he and the supposed customer had parked the Lincoln Continental outside the hall. Paul arrived breathless, offering apologies for his late appearance and stating that he was pretty sure that he had a buyer who was going to retrieve a cashier's check from the bank to buy the Continental. Paul was very pleased!

As Paul sat down to begin folding his stack of bulletins, he glanced through the window. Looking outside he couldn't see the Lincoln where it had been parked. He stood up to get a better view and then said with alarm, "THE LINCOLN'S NOT THERE! IT'S GONE!!!"

Before his retirement Paul had worked with the US Postal Service as an investigative detective in their criminal department. He was a professional Investigator. He rushed outside with obvious concern and when he returned Paul covered his face with his hands and groaned.

"OH, NO!! OF ALL PEOPLE-- I SHOULD HAVE KNOWN BETTER!!"

You see, after allowing the prospective customer to drive the car for several miles, they returned and parked the car outside the church. The customer announced that he was going for a cashier's check in order to buy the car, but then the man asked if he could just take a minute to inspect the trunk. Paul waited until the man took a look in the trunk and then the man returned the keys. Paul then hurried into the Fellowship Hall to help with the folding of the bulletins.

"OLDEST TRICK IN THE WORLD!" Paul muttered. You see as the thief had taken the keys from the ignition and walked back around the car to open the trunk. Once out of view, he slipped the ignition key from the key ring and pocketed it. Then after pretending to inspect the trunk he returned the key ring to Paul- minus one key. Of course it was the ignition key.

Believe it or not, the classy Lincoln Continental with the Continental Kit had been stolen right out from under retired detective Paul Alfred's eyes. But that wasn't the end of the story. The story continued with the subsequent police search for the car.

The Continental was found that same day parked at a Cadillac Agency down below the High Desert in the city of Riverside. The Lincoln was undamaged and still in mint condition. The thief had driven the Lincoln to the Cadillac Agency in Riverside and left both the Lincoln and a counterfeit driver's license as collateral for the new Cadillac that the Agency salesman had allowed the customer to take for a drive all by himself. Unfortunately, the potential buyer was a thief. He had traded up, and now in addition to the Lincoln Continental the Cadillac was also stolen!!!

However, by the end of the very next day the Cadillac was also found. It had been abandoned in the parking lot of the Gambling Casino in the nearby town of Adelanto. It turned out that the Cadillac, too, was undamaged and in mint condition. The police determined that between the two cars the thief had driven them over 600 miles. For two days he had sat behind the wheels of a vintage Lincoln Continental and then a brand new Cadillac – JOY RIDING! When the facts of the second theft were reported, everyone conjectured about kind of luck the man had encountered at the Casino???

I don't remember that the thief was ever caught, but believe me that first day of the Rummage Sale when the news spread and when Paul Alfred showed up to report back for duty in the Big Items Department, he was razzed and soundly roasted by all of the men involved in that department. They hailed him good naturedly as the Church of the Valley's most highly skilled Detective and most highly regarded Professional Investigator!!!!!!

But the story did have a very happy ending when Paul Alfred was able to sell the returned Lincoln Continental for a very handsome price!!! The sum significantly enhanced the mission outreach of the Church.

IT WAS THE DAY OF THE INGENIOUS RUSE IN APPLE VALLEY.

The Case of the Purloined Pipes
Art French

When I became the pastor of the First Presbyterian Church of Gardena, CA., I soon became aware of the congregation's great pride in their pipe organ. Any number of people told me of their effort in raising a considerable sum of money, well over a hundred thousand dollars. The organ had undergone an extensive overhaul and upgrade with several new stops. And wasn't it a great achievement. And didn't I just love its rich tone. And wasn't it a tremendous addition to our worship experience. And on and on. While everyone seemed so enthusiastic about the reconditioned organ, there was one person who was not – Freddie Lou McGinnis. Though a definite minority of one, Freddie Lou was not quiet about her growing displeasure with our organ.

Freddie Lou was our organist/choir director. Twice a week she drove down to the South Bay from her home in Northridge for Thursday night choir practice and Sunday morning worship. She was an exceptionally fine musician and our choir responded accordingly. I have always been interested in music and joined the choir in which I sang every Sunday. On occasion I would sing a solo from the pulpit to accompany some line of thought in a particular sermon. Therefore, I was in close and constant contact with Freddie Lou.

Soon it became very apparent to me that Freddie Lou was, to say the least, not at all happy or satisfied with the sound of the organ. Time and again she voiced her displeasure to me. *"How could this be?"* I questioned. "This organ had just had an expensive overhaul to make it sound better. "

Finally, somewhat in desperation for fear of losing a very fine musician, I approached the Session with the problem and requested authorization to engage several well-known and highly respected organ building firms to come and inspect our instrument and render their learned opinion as to the state of our organ. We contacted two such firms who sent representatives who looked and then gave their shocking reply that "Yes, the organ could be fixed." It would take $60,000 in one quote and $80,000 in the other. Neither of which could remotely be considered in our present financial situation.

My idea had backfired and we were no closer to solving our problem than before we started. However, it did confirm that Freddie Lou was right. Something was the matter with the organ!

Finally, I began to wonder who had done the work on the organ and if he was still available. He was not, but we learned that his assistant, Dick Muench, who had worked with him on our organ's renovation was still in the area and doing organ maintenance. Dick was contacted and agreed to come and look at the organ.

I will never forget the day he arrived and he and I entered the first pipe chamber through the outside door. As soon as Dick entered the room, with me close behind, his very first words were, "Where are the new pipes?"

I said "What do you mean, 'Where are the new pipes?' There are no pipes missing. Every row of pipes is full."

Dick answered my astonished question by replying, "See the pipes with the red collars?"

"Yes", I replied, still mystified.

He continued, "See where the red collars end and the rest of the pipes have no red collars?"

"Yes", I said.

"Well, the pipes with the red collars are the new pipes I installed. They should continue for the whole row. The pipes with no red collars are old pipes replacing the new ones."

To my incredulous, dumbfounded question "How can that be?" he told this story, apparently well-known in organ maintenance circles. Rumor had it that the church's contract organ maintenance man had stolen the new pipes, replacing them with old pipes from some Catholic church in Santa Monica. Then he put our new pipes into his organ which he was building in his garage right there in Gardena!

Of course, I was almost speechless! When the elders found out, it didn't take long to decide to report the theft to the Gardena Police Department. This turned out to be grand theft (anything over $2000). In a week or so, I received a call from the Police Department saying they had my pipes and would I come to pick them up. I drove my station wagon over there as fast as I could and collected the purloined pipes.

We figured out that with the change of pastors and organists no one would pay any attention to our contract organ maintenance man who had his own keys to do his work and could come and go at any time of the day or night. With no missing pipes, the organ still played.

Freddie Lou's ears knew the difference.

We hired Dick Muench to put the new pipes back and re-tune the organ. He became our new contract organ maintenance man for many years.

I went to court to testify. The man got off with some sort of plea bargain and soon after moved out of state.

Recently, when I told this story to a friend who is a long time and very active member of the local theater organ restoration and preservation society, his rather laconic reply was, "Oh, that has been known to happen."

Today
Ken Grant

We sometimes act
As if "then" was
A time apart
Disconnected from all other
Days and times
By an unseen wall
As though what happened
"Way back then"
Doesn't really matter any more
Or is
Inconsequential
In the drama of a vigorous
Today

Yet
Such a disconnect is clearly
A wishful dream
For the very stuff
Today is made of
In reality
Is but the residue of
All our yesterdays
Passing on through time's
Swift revolving door
The building blocks
Which
You and I
Trusting in God's love and aid
May assemble our today
Opening the way
To construct a more just
And beautiful
Tomorrow

ABOUT THE AUTHORS

Robert and Carole Bos:

We were raised in Michigan and met at Hope College. Bob has served five churches in Chicago and Southern California. Carole taught English and social studies in middle schools. We have been formulating a personal history book for our daughter and are pleased for the opportunity to add our six life stories to the kaleidoscope of colors for this book.

Bruce Calkins:

Then: Inner-city Pastor in the Bronx, NYC. Consultant to church institutions, boards, and Catholic religious communities. Interim Pastor in PA, NJ, and CA.

Now: Looking for the next open door (and trying not to walk into the door.) Father of four, husband of one.

Sometime: Wondering, whether I can help start some new churches or other ministry units? Wondering if I can and will climb Mt. Wilson on my 90th birthday.

Hobbies (and things I did a few times and like to think of as hobbies. This is relevant to some of my stories.) Hiking, cracking a bull whip, tomahawk throwing, and knife throwing.

Whenever: Once when I was traveling, I went to bed with many thoughts and questions going through my mind. I gave the questions to God and went to sleep. As I awoke, before opening my eyes, these words were going through my head"

"Before there were any yesterdays, I knew you."
I repeated the words over and over with my eyes closed so I would not forget them. Then I thought, "That's about the back half of eternity; what about the eternity of the future?" As I lay still with my eyes closed, these words came:

"After there are no more tomorrows, I will hold you."

I repeated the words over and over, then opened my eyes and wrote them down. That was a gift given to me. Now I give it to you.

Howard Den Hartog:

My wife, Esther, and I both graduated from Central College located in Pella, Iowa. Esther's father married us in the Pella Reformed Church near Panama, Nebraska in 1958. In 1971 I received a Master of Science degree from Forth Hays State University in Hays, Kansas. I have taught school in Iowa, Arizona, New Mexico, and Alabama. In 1964 we went as missionaries under the Board of Domestic Missions of the Presbyterian Church (USA) to Wasatch Academy in Mt. Pleasant, Utah where we served for twenty five years. We have four grown children who live in California, Utah, Oregon, and Washington.

Art & Carolyn French:

Art French was born in China of Presbyterian missionary parents and lived there 10 years, receiving home-schooling until fifth grade. He graduated from Wooster college in 1953, then attended Princeton Seminary. At the end of two years he went to Kings Lake Camp in Alaska and then spent a year providing spiritual care to the Presbyterian Church in Wasilla and other communities along the Alaska railroad. Then he returned to finish his last year of seminary.

Carolyn was born in Ohio and raised in Oak Park, Illinois, the daughter of a Lutheran Pastor. She attended two years at Wooster College and then went into a nursing program at the University of Pennsylvania and received her Bachelor of Science in Nursing (BSN). She then worked for the Denver Colorado Public Health Nursing Service for five months, returning to Pennsylvania where she & Art married in June 1957, two weeks following his ordination.

Two weeks later they were on their way to the mission field on St. Lawrence Island, Alaska about 40 miles from Siberia where one could see the Siberian Mountains on a clear day. Carolyn was hired by the Alaskan Territorial Department of Health as the only medical person on the Island of two villages 60 miles apart. They remained 6 years and had two of their 3 children during that time. They were there "at the end of an era" during which travel was by dog team in winter and skin boat in summer along with plane service twice monthly (weather permitting, pilot willing), to only the western most village with a metal matting airstrip on which to land.

From there they went to Idyllwild, California Community Presbyterian Church in a mountain community for six years and then to the First Presbyterian Church of Gardena for 30 years prior to retirement at MVG.

Mary Froede:

I lived my young life and had my schooling in Wisconsin. Married, had two children and went off to seminary with my husband who ended up being a Presbyterian minister for 42 years until his death. Jim's first job was Assistant Pastor in Beverly Hills. Our 3rd child joined the family while we were there. I still operate a full time business manufacturing vinyl aprons and tablecloths for restaurants in the entire USA (Taco Bell for one).

I have written a book telling of my family's experiences serving a church in Tucumcari, New Mexico in the '50s. Had great fun singing the music of the 40's with big bands (one of which was the Stan Kenton revival band). I am 83 years old, have seven grandchildren and six great grandbabies. I have loved being here at Monte Vista Grove for my final years.

Sherman Fung:

A native of San Francisco, I was born in 1925. I was educated by the Chinatown public grade school, junior high school in the Italian district, Commerce High School near Automobile Row, University of California at Berkeley, Dubuque Theological Seminary (Iowa), Wheaton Graduate School of Theology (Illinois), Educational Media Department of Bowling Green State University (Ohio). I worked for San Francisco City and County Department of Social Service; served overseas in Presbyterian Church, USA related projects as well as those of the Evangelical Church of Iran. Before retirement, I did audio visual services work at two higher education institutions in California. I've seen, heard, read, thought a lot, and talked about a lot of things over the decades. There are still a lot of gaps in knowledge, in understanding, and in opportunities and challenges to be filled. I'm hoping the next decade provides the time and space to do so.

Mae Gautier:

Mae lived all her early years in Miami where her family members were "pioneers", arriving in Miami in 1896 before the city was incorporated. Her father, uncles, and grandparents had floated on a barge down the inland waterway from Crescent City, Florida. After graduating from Florida State University and Vanderbilt University School of Theology, Mae was a Methodist campus minister at Iowa State University and at the University of South Carolina. She lived and worked in New York City during the next twenty-six years, in the administration at Union Theological Seminary and as Organizer for Peace and Justice Actions for the Presbytery of New York City. Mae moved to Pasadena and Monte Vista Grove in 1998. She is married to Norman E. Thomas, also an author in this book.

Kenneth Grant:

Kenneth E. Grant (Ken) was born in Los Angeles, California and raised in nearby Glendale. After attending Occidental College and serving a stint in the U.S. Navy in WWII, Ken graduated from USC. He attended both Princeton and San Francisco seminaries and has served churches in California and the Mid West. He and his wife, Beverly, became residents of Monte Vista Homes in 1994. He continues to preach and teach in his retirement and enjoys writing and oil painting.

Ken is perhaps best known for his portrayal of an old "cow poke" named Cactus who has been "guest preacher" in churches where he has served and for various organizations.

Bill Hansen:

Bill is a native Californian who grew up on the beaches of Southern California. He was educated at Occidental College and San Francisco Theological Seminary. Bill is the husband of Mary Ellen to whom he has been married 60 years. He is a father, a grandfather, and a great grandfather. He served his first pastorate in Kansas and served the remainder of his ministry for 40 years with the Church of the Valley, Presbyterian in Apple Valley, California.

Hedwig Lodwick:

Robert (Bob) and Hedwig (Hedy) were employed by the Presbyterian Church (USA) in their overseas missions. They were Fraternal Workers with the French Reformed Church (1953-1958) and Mission Co-Workers in Egypt with the Coptic Evangelical Church (1961 - 1964). From 1964 - 1978, they lived in New Jersey while Bob was Program Director for Education, responsible for the church's schools and colleges on 6 continents. During this time, Hedy taught pre-school. From 1978 - 1993 they represented the Presbyterian Church (USA) in Europe, with headquarters in Geneva, Switzerland. Bob was the Presbyterian Area Representative and Hedy worked extensively with Swiss and European Christian Women.

Barbara Mathieu:

I grew up in Los Angeles, attending L.A. High School and UCLA, where I completed my PhD in Anthropology. I taught at Loyola Marymount University in the 1980s and then full time for the Los Angeles Community College District from 1990-2005. Jim Mathieu and I married in 1960, have three sons and 6 grandchildren. We've lived and taught in Zambia, Lesotho, Mexico, Germany and Sikkim.

Jim, born in Pennsylvania, was a pastor when we married, and in the 70s after earning his PhD at USC, he taught Sociology at Loyola Marymount University for 34 years. Our teaching has afforded us to live in many places around the world. We moved to MVGHs in mid-January 2016, from our home of 52 years in West Los Angeles.

Laura Berthold Monteros:

I am a writer. I once read that if one really wants to become a professional writer, she should not say things like, "I want to be a writer" or "I'm trying to write." So I am a writer and have been since I was a child. I've been a journalist, a stay-at-home mom, and a secretary, and currently I write articles about the Tournament of Roses. For the class at the Grove, I write reminiscences, rants, reveals. And someday, I will dust off all those unpublished children's books I wrote for my kids.

219

Rosemary Pierson:

A native Californian, I grew up in beautiful San Luis Obispo. While a student at UC Berkley, I met Paul Pierson. After marriage we spent seventeen years as Presbyterian missionaries in Brazil and Portugal, followed by a pastorate in Fresno, Ca. In 1980 we moved to Pasadena where Paul served as Dean and professor at Fuller Theological Seminary. Our daughter, three sons, their spouses, and nine grandchildren bring us great joy.

Gloria Shamblin:

I was born in London during World War 2. My mother had been widowed 6 months previously when my father's RAF fighter plane had been shot down over the Zuider Zee in Holland. We did not evacuate but lived with family members. In 1948 my mother remarried and we moved to the coastal town of Bognor Regis. I grew up living over the family grocery store. I moved back to London for college years. I taught high school in London.

After a couple of years I moved to Pasadena California and worked as a nanny. I subsequently held many jobs, mainly in the medical field. I married and had 2 sons and 2 grandchildren. I currently live in Altadena.

Norman E. Thomas:

Norm joined the MVGH community in December 2006 after marriage to Grove resident Mae Gautier. A native of New Hampshire, he graduated from Yale University with A.B. and M. Div. degrees, and Boston University with a Ph.D. in Social Ethics and Sociology of Religion. An ordained United Methodist minister, Norm served as a pastor in Portland, Oregon, and as a missionary for fifteen years in Southern Africa (Rhodesia, now Zimbabwe, and Zambia). Later he taught missions, evangelism and church renewal, ecumenics, and world religions successively at Boston University and United Theological Seminary (Dayton, Ohio). Norm is the father of eight children (including four foster children from Zimbabwe), and grandfather of 26 with 3 great-grandchildren. He has authored and edited fourteen books and numerous articles on missions.

K. Roberta Woodberry:

Born and raised in the Midwest, our family finally settled in St. Paul, Minnesota where my Dad (Dr. Bob Smith) taught at Bethel College. I was the eldest of five children. We were privileged to spend our summers traveling all over the United States and then internationally accompanying my Dad, who was a well-known preacher and teacher.

My Mom. a teacher and musician, made a loving home for us all--even as we travelled and eventually spent time overseas. Mom taught me piano and voice from the time I could barely reach the keyboard and I intended to follow that path. But during my junior year in college, our family moved to Lebanon where my Dad was teaching. It was during that time that I sensed the Lord's calling to serve Him in the Middle East and I switched my major to elementary education, but have continued to use my music.

It was in Beirut that I met Dudley. After finishing graduate school we served together in Pakistan, Afghanistan, Saudi Arabia, Michigan and California.

We were blessed with three sons. As a stay-at-home Mom for 20 years, I was able to still teach, direct adult and children's choirs at church and school and provide a home for my family in some difficult places.

With two of our sons in college, I began teaching full-time again at Pasadena Christian School and then at Valentine School in San Marino. Subsequently I taught in Peshawar, Pakistan. (We were there on 9/11) and in Kabul, Afghanistan.

In 2011, Dudley and I moved from our home in Altadena to Monte Vista Grove Homes.

Made in the USA
San Bernardino, CA
08 September 2016